I0487431

If You Want To Be Rich,
Don't Buy This Book

If You Want To Be Rich, Don't Buy This Book

Rich E. Obscure

iUniverse, Inc.
New York Lincoln Shanghai

If You Want To Be Rich, Don't Buy This Book

iUniverse books may be ordered through booksellers or by contacting:

iUniverse
2021 Pine Lake Road, Suite 100
Lincoln, NE 68512
www.iuniverse.com
1-800-Authors (1-800-288-4677)

ISBN-13: 978-0-595-37233-1 (pbk)
ISBN-13: 978-0-595-81631-6 (ebk)
ISBN-10: 0-595-37233-3 (pbk)
ISBN-10: 0-595-81631-2 (ebk)

Printed in the United States of America

Contents

Introduction

This is a book about personal finance, as if there weren't enough of them already. There will be books about personal finance in the future, too, because you, the consumer, are always hungry for information that can make you rich. I'd like to be rich, too, just like the next guy.

That's right, you read correctly—I want to be rich.

"Wait one minute," you might be saying. "You aren't rich? How can you possibly write a book about personal finance and getting rich if you aren't rich?"

That's a valid question, and I'll answer it with another question. Why do you think someone who is rich will help you more? I've read books by people who were rich (and smart) but they didn't make me rich, and a lot of them didn't even contain much useful information. Some authors fill page after page with the same tired clichés surrounded by cute anecdotes that don't do anything to illustrate a financial point, and think they have written a book that's worth your hard-earned money.

If you're going to buy a book on personal finance, you will probably expect the author to offer advice you can use. Whether the author is rich or merely doing well, what's important is that you get advice with practical applications in the real world. Incidentally, if your definition of rich is to have over a million dollars, while still in your early 30s, then I am rich. However, I don't think of myself as rich, because I still need to work and I'm constantly striving to do better.

I have a *not*-so-well-kept secret. It's hard to become rich. I know, I didn't want to believe it either, but the evidence is clear, and statistics don't lie. (They don't always tell the truth, but they don't lie.) Only 5 percent of U.S. households make more than $200,000 a year. Sure that's a lot of money, but are these people really rich? I suppose it depends on what your definition of rich is.

I think someone is rich if they have more money than I do, but that's just me. According to the IRS, in order to be considered among the top 5 percent of taxpayers, you would have to have an adjusted gross income over $128,000 a year. That's a nice income, but is it really enough to make you rich? To be considered in the top 1 percent, you would need over $313,000 a year in income. There's a big difference between those numbers, but I'm thinking more about the people we see every day who make millions—the actors and actresses we are so consumed with, the musicians whose homes we see on *MTV Cribs*, the athletes signing multi-million-dollar contracts that lead to even larger multi-million-dollar endorsement deals. Then there are the businesspeople like Bill Gates, the richest man in the world, or the CEOs of other large companies, who are among the truly rich. For example, Michael Eisner, the former CEO of Disney, exercised over $500,000,000 in stock options in 1998. That's half a billion dollars. These people are the true rich we all think of when we hear that word. These are the people we think we most want to be like. Do you really think that reading a personal finance book (no matter who the author is) is going to make you rich in that sense of the word?

So the question remains: what is rich? Well I'm going to take the easy way out and say that depends on you. It's up to you to decide what your goal is. I hope this book, and the other resources I'll give you, will help you reach that goal.

As I said earlier, this book is different from the personal finance books I've read, because I offer practical and useful suggestions. I want you to be able to read my advice and put it into practice. In order for you to do this, I have made my suggestions clear, concise, and concrete so you can apply them immediately—with no money, no assets, and little work (at least in the beginning).

My approach is perhaps a bit unorthodox. I don't want to bore you, and I especially don't want to waste your time with empty words. My writing style is casual, because I want you to think of this book as a friend you can sit down and discuss your finances with. (Just don't let anyone see you do that.) It's my intention that one thing lead to the other in this book, so ignoring one item can result in total disaster. Well maybe that's overstating things a bit, but it's true that each element, each suggestion, is more powerful when used in conjunction with the others.

One more note before we move on: I'd like to apologize to my wife and the other people who, over the years, have put up with my schemes. I've talked incessantly about my grand dreams and the next big deal that would make me rich. I was going to write, direct, and produce movies. I was going to open a health club, a restaurant, and a non-profit organization, among other things. I was going to buy and sell real estate, too, but everyone seems to be doing that these days.

Imagine if your wife, husband, brother, or sister came to you and said they were going to write a book. You might think they were nuts, but with me, people got used to this and maybe I infected them because sometimes, like with this book, they would actually encourage me.

When it came to money and finances, I got it. I understood the concepts, applied them, and did fairly well. I studied by reading books on the subject (most of which disappointed me) and watching CNBC (where I sort of worked for a while). To make the leap and actually write a book on the subject seemed presumptuous on my part, but I have seen too many people struggle with their finances, and if this book can help even one person then it is worth it to me.

I do hope you enjoy the book. Without any more delay, let's begin with a bit of fun.

1

Just Like the Rest?

Welcome to my book. Since you're reading these words, I can assume a couple of things. The first is that you bought the book, which tells me you just don't have what it takes to be rich. I mean here was some advice—free advice—that could have kept twenty bucks in your pocket—and you didn't take it. If you want to be rich, don't buy this book! What could be simpler?

If I had walked up to you and handed you twenty dollars would you take it? I thought you would. But the words on the cover of this book—big words (well mostly big), weren't enough. Perhaps you borrowed the book from someone else, maybe even a library. If this is the case, you are on your way to riches! Of course, you have to return the book, otherwise you would be stealing, and while you might get rich, you wouldn't feel good about yourself, and that's important too.

You know, I am serious about the title of this book. I expected my publisher to be angry that I insisted on this title. If people actually listened to my advice and kept away from this book in droves, the publisher wouldn't make any money—in droves. This means I wouldn't make any money either, but that's okay—I won't lose sleep over it. Actually, I did self-publish the book, so part of me **is** losing sleep but the other part just doesn't care.

In this book, you'll find many "what ifs"—what if you won the lottery, for example. Use your imagination. ***You aren't going to get rich by thinking logically***. That is my first piece of advice—was that worth twenty bucks? Well, there's more where that came from (and I'll expand on this one later)! You're going to find little catch phrases like this throughout the book. They will appear in bold and italics so that you will remember them and pass them on to others. The bolding was a flash that just came to me, and I went with it. ***Go with your gut***. That's what I do, and you should do it too because it's printed in bold italics.

This is the kind of information you just can't come up with on your own. You're just not smart enough. You absolutely need someone like me to tell you. Deep down, you might know that your instincts are usually right, but when it comes to getting rich, do you really listen? You also might know that buying that fancy new Porsche isn't the wisest choice considering your mortgage eats up 80 percent of your salary and your credit cards are maxed out, but it's a real nice car, and, after all, you tell yourself, you deserve it. You need someone like me to point out subtle and intricate financial facts of life such as live within your means!

Live within your means. I was thinking of printing that in bold and italics, but that just doesn't have the same pizzazz as *Go with your gut*. What matters these days is what sounds good. You see examples of it every day. I mean, who would buy a car if the slogan was "plain but cheap"? No one, that's who. However, plenty of people buy Mazdas, whose slogan is "Zoom Zoom" and that sounds cool to me.

I think the main obstacle to getting rich is refusing to roll the dice. Take a risk! You see the fear of risk everywhere, including professional investments. People invest in stocks and mutual funds all the time, and printed somewhere in the mutual fund prospectus are the words "Past performance is no indication of future profits…." Blah, blah, blah. There's a reason that is printed so small. That is just some lawyer telling the mutual fund company to play it safe, but you want to be rich, and *safe is the enemy of rich.*

The United States is full of stories of people who have taken great risks and ended up successful and powerful—George Washington, Abraham Lincoln, and Martha Stewart are just a few. Sure Martha has her problems now that she's a convicted felon, but when she got out of jail, she was still filthy rich, so I'd say things aren't so bad for her. Fine, Abraham Lincoln got killed, but look at how history loves him. We also have great sales because of Lincoln and Washington, and sales are good. Not only that, but we get President's Day off to shop at those sales.

Sales are an important stepping-stone to wild riches. Let's say you really want a plasma screen TV but can't even come close to affording it. Don't get all depressed and feel sorry for yourself—just wait for a sale. Instead of paying $5,000, you may be able to get it for just $4,500—that's a savings of $500! Who cares if you still can't afford the $4,500. At least you saved $500. That's like money in the bank, right?

If you think small and let little things like a lack of money stop you, then give up. If there's anything I've learned from watching infomercials and reading get-rich-quick books, it's that getting rich doesn't take any money at all—at least not your own. You can buy houses for no money down or place small classified ads in small newspapers—it's that easy! The key word is *leverage.*

James K. Glassman and Kevin Hassett wrote a book called *Dow 36,000*. In it, they say that the Dow Jones Industrial average will be at 36,000 soon. What that tells me is that I should put every last penny of my savings into stocks, since they're a sure thing. ***If it's in a book, it must be true***. Who cares that since *Dow 36,000* was written, the stock market has virtually crashed and six years later is just now reaching its highs again. The secrets to wealth and power are printed for everyone to see. You just have to be willing to go for it. Oh yeah, and you have to believe it.

Imagine if in 1990, when the Dow Jones Industrial Average was around 2,700 (it really was), some idiot came out with a book titled *Dow 11,000*. He or she would have been laughed right into oblivion, but that person would have been right. In May 1999, the Dow did indeed reach that incredible level. Would my fake book, written in 1990 have been proved right and the author vindicated? No—he still would have been an idiot.

I'm not saying that either James Glassman or Kevin Hassett is an idiot. Actually, they are smarter than I will ever be. Glassman is a columnist for the *Washington Post* and Hassett was an economist for the Federal Reserve. I can't compete with them, and if you put the three of us in a debate, I'd lose miserably. Having said that, someone has to hold them accountable for their reckless title. I think they were just cashing in on the frenzy that was the stock market in the late 1990s.

Surely, there are good sources of information out there. Actually, there are so many ways to get rich or retire early that people are writing books, making infomercials, and even going on QVC just to give you the information. These people are modern-day saints, because their only concern is that you have a better life tomorrow than the one you have today. Of course, the more books they sell, the better they will do, but hey, that's the way the system works, and who are we to deny them that? I'm taking your money after all, and I'm here to help.

Screeeech…

That's the sound of this train wreck coming to a stop. Enough fun. What you have just read is how I think other people think of you. They think you will buy anything they are selling, that you're gullible. Some of the advice you get might actually look like some of the idiotic things I've said so far. You might have actually bought something that you didn't need just because it was on sale, thinking you saved money. You didn't, however; you would have saved more if you hadn't bought it at all—that's common sense.

Some of the things I have just said have some basis in truth, but be careful! The advice **Go with your gut** doesn't tell you much, but sometimes you just get a feeling and you know it's right. Intuition is important, but it can be dangerous. **Safe is the enemy of rich** seems reasonable too; after all, the greater the risk, the greater the chance for reward, but that doesn't mean that everything you do should be risky. There are ways to make a risky situation safer, in other words, to take a "calculated risk."

This book is not like all the rest. I don't use empty clichés that sound good but leave you wondering how to apply them. Clearly, a current popular and best selling author of finance books is Robert Kiyosaki. When I first began searching for honest reviews of his books, all I found were positive ones, yet I knew this was just another in a long line of books to make you feel good or make you spend more money attending his seminars, where you don't learn anything practical. Finally, I found a thorough and honest article in the February 2003 issue of *Smart Money* magazine.

On the title page of the article, "Karma Chameleon," Eleanor Laise begins by saying, "When it comes to details on his strategies—and on his background—this New Age sensation proves mighty slippery." I can only hope that no one ever calls me a "new age sensation" (or "mighty slippery" for that matter). The article does an excellent job of picking Mr. Kiyosaki apart, at one point describing the author's general approach: "Wrapping his words in a hodgepodge of New Age philosophy (wealth, he likes to say, is a 'spiritual quest'), he describes strategies in only the most abstract terms, and his advice is often contradictory and confusing."

Imagine buying a book to learn the secrets to early retirement and reading the following: "It's not about how. It is about why Kim and I did it…Without the why, the how would have been impossible. *I could go on to tell you how I did it, but I won't. How we did it is not that important.*" [from *Retire Young, Retire Rich*, by Robert Kiyosaki, emphasis added.]

Explain to me why he won't tell you, the reader, the one who spent the money to learn this very information, how to do it. Isn't that the whole point? Well I would tell you how to do it—if I only knew how. The best I can do is give you my opinion, but isn't that all any of these books offer? The title of *The Laws of Money*, by Suze Orman, sounds like it will give you facts, but "one size fits all" advice just isn't possible. (Sorry, Suze.) "One size fits most" advice may work, but it's up to you to apply the information to your specific situation. The good news is that common sense still works, as long as you modify the information for your particular needs.

I make lists to remind me of what I need at the supermarket, but no list is going to help you get rich. There aren't five, ten, or twenty rules for success—there are no rules. There are no twelve steps to riches. You make your own rules, and if they work for you, great, but that doesn't mean they will work for the next guy. Bill Gates never finished college, opting instead to start his own business, but that doesn't mean college is a waste of time. His method worked for him, but it won't necessarily work for you or me.

If you have a mortgage and your interest rate is 8 percent and rates drop to 6 percent, I'd say the advice to refinance is probably a good one (one size fits all) but do you refinance for thirty years, twenty years, or fifteen years? This detail is the personalized part only you or someone you trust enough to give your entire financial picture can determine. The general rule is to reduce the term of the mortgage, but that might not be possible in your case.

You are smarter than most people give you credit for, but the truth is that you lack confidence. I don't even know you, but I would bet I'm right. You think you need someone to tell you what to do or how to get rich quick when you know the reality is that you are probably doing just fine and that there are no quick answers. If you think buying a book or ordering a package from an infomercial is going to make you the next Bill Gates or Warren Buffet, you need to go to the bathroom and splash cold water on your face.

I hope that the words in this book will give you the confidence to do the right thing, and that might mean doing less or having less (for a little while). The greatest lesson anyone can learn is that in order to get what you want, **you have to work at it**. Unfortunately, there is just no way around that truth. You have to have discipline and the will to do without something now to get more later.

The plethora of finance books out there today have been written by more qualified people than myself, so why are you reading this? Why didn't you pick a book that some "expert" wrote? The reason is that common sense is not the exclusive domain of the experts—you and I have it, but we just need to use it more. It's a sad statement that common sense just isn't that common. The other reason is that "past performance is no indication" that you will do the same thing. In other words, the mere fact that some man or woman wrote a book doesn't mean that reading it will make you as successful as they are, and that goes for this one too.

Donald Trump's Apprentice contestants Bill Rancic, Amy Henry and Anthony Parinello have all written business success books. Fellow contestants Heidi Bressler and Troy McClaine are either writing or have been asked to write a book. How were these people qualified to write a book? If they weren't on the show, would they have been signed to a book deal at all?

The true measure of success is making do with a small amount of money, not making a million dollars a year. I thought *The Millionaire Next Door,* by Thomas J. Stanley and William D. Danko, was a great title for a book, because it's not always obvious who the wealthy are. My wife and I drove eleven-year-old cars, because we just didn't see why we should spend a lot of money on a new car when we had two working vehicles. Sure, I wanted almost every new car out there but I didn't need them. The difference between need and want is an important distinction, and he who masters that is doing all right.

2

Why Is It So Hard?

Managing money doesn't seem difficult on the surface, and it's easy for someone to give you advice, but how do you know you can trust that person? That's a big concern when the person giving you the advice is a complete stranger. But hey you bought the book so there must be some reason you trust me.

My goal in this chapter is to wake you up. I want to tell you that it's not really that hard, even though so many people seem to have trouble figuring out the simple truth that you need to save, you need to have fun without going broke, and you need to do this now. You can't wait till you're so deep in debt that the remedy is painful. If it's already too late, then the advice in this chapter won't be easy, but you *can* follow it, and if you want a life without fear and stress, you *will* start now.

I must admit that although this is the intent of this chapter, I've become disillusioned. I have heard people say things like "I have so many late fees because I just can't pay my bills on time." One such person, when I asked her why she had late fees, said, "Well, there are so many bills that I put them down and lose them or find them after the due date." I was shocked. It is one thing if an individual is overextended and simply doesn't have enough money to cover the various bills. That would not be okay but it is at least understandable. But to let disorganization or laziness cost you late fees, higher interest rates, and bad credit is stupid. This person deserves the trouble she is in, and even though she will blame everyone else, the fault lies with her. If you are one of these people, understand that you need to fix yourself. You don't need to fix the credit card companies. They aren't broken, but you are.

If you are so far gone that you pay your bills late or transfer debt from one credit card to the other just to stay a little ahead, my message for you is to take responsibility for your actions. No one caused this but you. It's no one else's fault that you don't make enough money. It's no one else's fault that you fell on hard times. It might not be your fault either—maybe you lost your job due to outsourcing or the slow economy—but whether you dealt with that situation promptly and responsibly was entirely up to you. If you continued spending as if you were employed, you have no one to blame but yourself.

I'm disillusioned, because I think some people just can't be helped. They can read this book, and hundreds of others, but it won't do them any good. Don't be this person. The help is out there, in the form of books, lectures, and advice from friends and professionals, but if you don't recognize that you need to change, then it won't do any good. Don't let this happen to you.

I have a friend who knows he lives paycheck to paycheck yet is unwilling to make even a small sacrifice to pull himself up a bit. He leases a car every two or three years, and so he will never be without a car payment. The four or five hundred dollars a month he spends can do much more for him in a bank account, a Certificate of Deposit (CD), or even the stock market (in spite of low interest rates and the stock market's slow progress back to the highs of the late 1990s).

The people who are struggling with money issues know how much money they make—it's certainly not a secret to them—yet they spend more than they have. It's certainly easy to get carried away, but why can't they stop themselves? Why is the average savings rate in the United States below zero (yes below zero) for 2005, when in 2002 it was 3.7 percent, while people in the European Union save 15 percent?

In 2002, there were 1,053,230 Chapter 7 personal bankruptcy filings. That's too many. The year 2003 was even worse, with 1,165,993 Chapter 7 personal bankruptcy filings, followed by 2004 with 1,167,101 and 2005 with 1,196,212. I understand the stock market lost a lot between 2000 and 2001, and that hurt many people. But did they do anything about it? Did they recognize the situation and take steps to make sure they wouldn't end up in deeper trouble? My guess is that they didn't.

Open the newspaper to the legal notices, and you'll see quite a few foreclosures listed every week. Why can't these people afford their homes? We all go through hard times, and there are events that we just can't foresee but I think it's poor planning, laziness, and unfortunately sometimes, sheer foolishness that causes a lot of these bankruptcies and foreclosures.

Spending should always lag income. *It just doesn't make sense to spend more than you make*, yet we buy everything on credit. Credit makes it very difficult to see whether you can really afford something or not. That's not to say that credit is a bad thing, but *not keeping track of spending certainly is a prelude to failure*.

When you become better at keeping your money and not falling behind in your bills, you'll want to keep doing better. You'll read more about money and how to save it, invest it, and spend it more wisely. Even with my level of success, I do this and I'm often shocked to see other people with such serious problems. I read an online forum about personal finance on the *Motley Fool* website, and I see people seeking advice about how to get out of debt. This is serious debt they're talking about—$50,000, $100,000, or even a "low" number like $10,000. And this is just credit card debt and doesn't include other items such as car loans, with which many people overextend themselves. The fact that they are on the *Motley Fool* forum, however, says a lot about their chances of getting out from under their pile of debt. They have taken the first step toward success.

I'm not so vain to think that I have all the answers. There are plenty of other resources out there for you to learn about finances. This book, in my humble opinion, is a great resource, but it definitely isn't the only one. The *Motley Fool* website is one I rely on every day, especially the forums, where real people like you and me give each other advice. You are never too smart to stop learning.

One of the biggest mistakes a person can make when thinking about money is to get into the "what-if" way of thinking. What if I get that raise or what if I get that new job—then I'll be able to afford it, so why not get it now? I had a friend who was convinced he was going to get a great settlement from a lawsuit. Even though the accident was his fault, he was convinced the manufacturer of the device that injured him would settle out of court rather than go to trial. My friend bought great stereo equipment, a new TV, and a really nice pickup truck, but the money never came. He knew exactly what to do *if* he got a settlement but not *if* he didn't. Wouldn't he have been wiser to plan *not to win* the settlement? We tend not to think that way, however, because we're all dreamers—we dream of riches, but we aren't willing to work for them.

Another common mistake is "double counting" or giving too much weight to a certain amount of money when deciding whether we can afford something. This happens more often than you might think. I'm guilty of it myself. Let's assume that I got a bonus at work of $5,000 (fat chance), and I needed $2,000 worth of repairs to my car. I'm in luck, since I can apply the bonus to the car and still have $3,000 left. My problem, however, is that I then say, "Hey why don't I buy that motorcycle I always wanted. It's just $4,500, and I just got a $5,000 bonus." Now I have just allocated $6,500 in spending using only $5,000 in income. I do this all the time, but I'm usually able to stop myself from buying the motorcycle or whatever extra luxury item that I want. It's the ability to restrain yourself that makes the difference. Just because I got a $5,000 bonus doesn't mean that I actually have $5,000 to spend. Here's another example: Let's say I have wanted to buy a new piece of furniture and it just happens to cost $4,500.

So after I learn about my $5,000 bonus, I go out and buy the furniture. But when the check comes in, it's only for $2,700. What happened? Taxes and other deductions—that's what happened—and if you don't take those into account, you aren't spending or allocating your money wisely.

Yet another mistake is ignoring expenses that you just can't ignore. You might say to yourself, "I make $4,000 a month, ($48,000 a year) so I can afford the new car at $450 a month and the mortgage of $1,500 a month and the gym membership of $100 (for a total of $2050 a month)." But the problem comes when you confuse gross income (before taxes) for net income (after taxes). What about the other deductions, such as health insurance, life insurance, and 401(k) contributions? These are real expenses that you just can't ignore. What about the smaller items that always add up, like food, utilities, and whatever hobbies you might have? What you make and what you take home are two different things, and understanding that difference, and living within the constraints in your life, is what determines if you'll have extra money to save or spend at the end of the month.

Believing you have more than you really do leads to more debt. The million-plus people who filed for bankruptcy in 2002 didn't think it would happen to them. They used their credit card for their gym memberships, groceries, and gas, and then paid the minimum every month (if they made every payment).

Because we have financial options, people think they can beat the system. You know the saying "A little bit of knowledge is a dangerous thing," right? Well, just because you think you have an idea that will save you money doesn't mean that it will or that you will save as much as you think. Good intentions followed by poor execution can be worse than not taking the action in the first place. You figure that since you have too much credit card debt, you'll just get a new card with a low introductory rate and transfer the balance. That's a good plan, but eventually that rate will go up, and in the meantime, if you're still spending like there's no tomorrow, you will go further into debt.

The same principle applies with large items, such as your home. With interest rates so low in recent years, people rushed to refinance their homes, which makes perfect financial sense. The problem is that many people did it for the wrong reasons and in the wrong way. Many people certainly didn't think their decision through. Assume you're paying $1,200 a month for the principal and interest (we'll ignore escrow, because you'll have to pay that anyway) and are ten years into a thirty-year mortgage (which means you only have twenty years left). You can refinance and save yourself a couple of hundred dollars a month by bringing your payments down to $1,000. If you refinanced for thirty years again, though, you've just added ten more years of interest payments.

The smarter choice would have been to choose a shorter-term mortgage such as a twenty or fifteen year. Your payment might not be any less, and in some cases (depending on the interest rate) it might even be slightly higher, but you will be saving an incredible amount of interest in the long run. If you take a loan for $150,000 for thirty years at 6 percent interest, your payment will be about $900 a month, with total interest payments over thirty years of $173,757. That's right—you are paying more in interest than the cost of the house. That same loan, however, with the same interest rate taken for only fifteen years will give you a payment of $1,265 a month, but the total interest over those fifteen years will be only $77,841. That's a huge savings of $95,915. That's almost a hundred thousand dollars that you will not have spent, but you don't see it, because all you can see is your larger monthly payment. That's called "short-term thinking," when our goal in life should be financial security in the long term.

The problem is, while people are paying less each month with the thirty-year refinance, they aren't *saving* the difference. Assume that because of the refinance, they are spending $150 less each month. If they take the opportunity to increase spending instead of saving that money, they aren't doing themselves any good, but that's exactly what people do. That is exactly how they got into trouble in the first place, and they will probably end up there again.

The other benefit of the reduced-term mortgage is that you pay off your principal much faster, thereby increasing your equity in the house. You may have ignored the savings in interest because you didn't intend to stay in the house for twenty or even fifteen years, but with the shorter-term mortgage, you'll get more in your pocket when you sell the house. It's a win-win situation no matter how you look at it.

Like I said, and will continue to say, sometimes the smarter choice, the one that will give you more options later, doesn't seem that way on the surface. It doesn't seem to make sense to pay more each month for your house if you can pay less. Imagine you decide to take the thirty-year mortgage, "saving" $365 a month. You could buy a nice car for that money, but remember that you are paying over $95,000 more over the thirty-year life of the mortgage. Now that buys a *really* nice car.

With home prices rising so quickly recently, people are also doing what's called a "cash out" refinancing. This is when you use the equity built up in the house to refinance more than you currently owe on the mortgage. There are many reasons why people do this, and most of them are bad. In order to do well financially, you have to use assets properly. A bank is a great place to store money and earn interest. Stocks are a great way to invest a small amount and, with luck, turn it into a large amount. You can't get great returns from the bank, but you also don't have the risk associated with the stock market. Each asset, or tool, has its purpose. This is also true of assets such as your home. Be careful, however. A house is not a bank, yet some people are using the incredibly low interest rates of the recent past to "withdraw" money from their homes.

Some people do it to pay off high-interest credit card bills. While it is true that you're getting rid of the worst kind of debt possible, it still isn't a great idea. There is a huge potential here for failure. This only works if you are disciplined enough never to have credit card debt again. If you're only going to continue to rack up the bills, you've made a terrible mistake, because now you will be paying those bills for thirty years, in your new mortgage, and adding more to the credit cards every day.

Even if you don't add any more debt to your cards, it might not be a good idea to roll the debt into the mortgage. Let's assume that you had $15,000 in credit card debt that you added to your refinance. Let's also assume that the interest on the credit cards was 14 percent and your new thirty-year mortgage is 6 percent. If you paid $200 per month toward reducing the credit card debt, you would pay it off in just over six years, with $7,643.12 spent in interest. But (there's always a but isn't there), the extra $15,000 in your mortgage would cost you $17,375.73 in interest over the thirty years. That wasn't a very smart idea, was it? Of course, if you had taken a fifteen-year mortgage, the amount of interest you would have added by rolling the credit card debt into the mortgage would have been $7,784.14 at the same 6 percent interest rate. Compared to the $7,643.12 you would have paid keeping the credit card debt, there's very little difference. The problem is that fifteen-year mortgages have higher monthly payments than thrity-year mortgages. If you refinanced with a fifteen-year mortgage, your monthly spending would have increased by more than the $200 you were paying toward your credit card debt. So rolling the credit card debt into a fifteen-year mortgage wasn't a smart idea either.

Some people take a "cash out" refinance because they want to make repairs to their house or build an addition. This can be a good idea, especially since home prices have appreciated so much. But don't get carried away. Drunk on the cash, you might be tempted to go overboard on the amenities, adding marble floors or granite countertops or maybe that entertainment system you've always wanted. That is not the road to riches. These items might look nice and might even increase the value of your home a bit, but not nearly as much as the money you have spent. If you can do without these luxuries now, you'll be that much further ahead later.

"But my house is my biggest and best investment," you protest, spouting the conventional wisdom. There are some who would agree with you (including me) and some who wouldn't. However, that doesn't mean you should go out and buy the biggest house you can find. Once you add all the costs of owning a home, the return is modest at best. There will be more on this later, but for now, suffice it to say that you must approach your home as cautiously as you would any other investment. Do your homework and use common sense.

I've mentioned the expression that a little bit of knowledge is a dangerous thing, right? Well it's especially true with money issues. All this talk of mortgages and refinancing in a chapter called "Why Is It So Hard" is meant to show you that by using financial tools available to all of us, you can improve your situation. The problem—and I hope the examples have illustrated this—is that taking advantage of some financial tool or trick is not enough. You must also plan for what you'll do after you have executed your smart move. If you follow the smart move with a dumb one or use a smart technique for dumb reasons, the whole thing is for naught.

I look at people who are struggling with money issues and see, to my surprise, that a lot of them make a decent living. You may be like that—maybe that's why you're reading this—or you might know someone who fits that description. What these people often lack is common sense. I would bet that if you asked yourself (or your friend with money troubles) what you could do to save more, you'd know the answer—spend less. We all know it's that simple, but we ignore the fact that even little things add up, justifying our purchases with comments like, "Oh it's just a couple of bucks. It won't kill me." It's the little things that make us wonder where all the money we got in our paychecks has gone.

Something as simple as buying a music CD every week can cost you $676 or more a year. Paying $3 a day for coffee can cost you over $1000 a year. Now imagine making your own coffee and saving $2 a cup—that's a savings of $730 a year. I bet you could find something to do with that money.

We can definitely save money by monitoring our vices. My father quit smoking back when cigarettes were just fifty cents a pack. As a reward for quitting, he put fifty cents a day into a jar, and at the end of the year had $182.50 to buy himself something nice (and since cigarettes were just fifty cents you know $182.50 probably bought something pretty good). With cigarette prices over $5 a pack, quitting would give you $1,825 or more at the end of the year, and you'd be healthier. Of course if you live in New York City you're paying over $7 a pack and that adds up to $2,555 a year, double that if you smoke two packs a day.

But it's not just the little things. There are bigger demons lurking. We all want to be successful, and what better way to display our success than to have nice things. A fancy car, a big house, top-notch stereo equipment, and other status-enhancing items are great ways to project a sense of prosperity. The problem is that none of this is helping you to become rich. If you can learn this lesson and be a bit more modest in your appearance, you are on your way to victory.

Managing money is hard because people often do what's quick, easy, and makes them feel good, giving themselves disadvantages instead of advantages. When people are just beginning their adult lives, financial mistakes can set a precedent that determines their financial future. How about a brief fairy tale? There once was a good-looking guy and a pretty girl who met one day in a park (sounds better than a bar). They fell in love—yes, it was love at first sight—and began talking about marriage in no time. They decided to get married in a year, and then they moved in together and began planning the wedding. Neither of their parents could help financially, but the couple wanted a day to remember, and so they decided to pay for it themselves. You know the rest: the expensive dress, the big rock of a diamond, the limousines, the 150 guests at $125 a head, and the 100 white doves released at just the right moment. Add all that up, and our two lovers had quite a large bill, which they couldn't actually afford. But don't worry—they put it on their credit card and would deal with it later.

Common sense is the key to success, but how many of us actually practice it? Those poor newlyweds certainly didn't. I have a family friend who occasionally goes to a casino to try her luck (not a strategy I would endorse). She takes the bus with the rest of her friends and rarely ever loses a lot. She has a system that I've loosely applied to my finances. Let's say she goes to the casino with $100. She takes her initial "investment" and puts it in her left pocket. As she plays her "games of chance," she uses only the money in that left pocket. When she wins, the winnings go into her right pocket, and she won't touch them until she's home. This way, she almost never loses it all.

I've taken my friend's casino system and applied it to my financial life. The difference is, I don't keep all my money in my pockets. Figuratively I do, as I keep my money in the bank, but I don't want to take this analogy that far. This system has changed the way I think about the money I have available to use on a daily basis. All my income goes into the bank (my right pocket). I take an allowance each week for cash purchases (the left pocket), and I don't spend beyond that. Sure, I stray once in a while, but nobody's perfect. Some weeks I don't use all the money, and I'm ahead of the game. Some weeks I use more, but I have to have a good reason.

An allowance is different from a budget. I don't have a budget, and I don't believe in them. If I have a budget that includes X dollars a month on CDs, I'll want to spend that each month whether I want the music or not. Alternatively, if I'm under budget on groceries, I'll want to splurge on luxury foods rather than save the extra. An allowance allows me to spend on whatever I want, as long as I don't go over the limit. When I want to make a big purchase or just treat myself, I know I'll have the money available, because I've been restrained in my daily life. This works whether you make $20,000 or $200,000 a year. The only difference is that the person who makes $200,000 has a much larger allowance.

This concept works only when you have a good handle on exactly how much money you have at any time as well as how much you make and spend. The key to this system is knowledge, and this can only come by carefully studying your finances. Keep track of everything so that you know exactly where your money is coming from and where it's going.

Why is this so hard? Because most people don't think about the things I've laid out in this chapter. Most people don't pay attention to their money. They may know they have problems, but they aren't willing to take the time to figure out why.

3

Keeping Records and Losing Debt

Okay, now we're going to get into the nitty-gritty, and it won't be pretty. We're going to look at charts and tables and graphs, and they are just as boring now as they were in school. That's an important concept but doesn't need to be printed in bold italics—graphs and charts are boring!

So far, I have found most of the you-can-be-rich-too books I've read really, really short on details. They spend pages and pages saying, "You can do it" and "Go for your dreams" and "Believe in yourself." They spout clichés and cute catch phrases, such as "Make your money work for you" or "Pay yourself first." However, they rarely actually give you any details, any real advice on what to do or how to do it. I'll tell you all these things too, because it is important that you are confident in your abilities, but I'm also going to tell you what has worked for me and for people who are more successful than I am. Will you be as successful as I am or as the others I hold up as examples in these pages? I don't know but at least it's a start and more of a start than you'll get from a lot of sources. And of course there are those who will read this and attain success greater than me or even most people—I hope that's you.

They say there are two kinds of people in the world, financially speaking: those who keep track of every penny and those who don't. The people who do keep detailed records of their finances are much more likely to have more than those who don't. If you know where your cash is coming from and where it's going, you should be able to manage it better. When times get tight, you can quickly and easily assess how best to make up for the change.

Suppose you have lost your job and have started collecting unemployment. Now that you don't have as much money as you did before, do you change your lifestyle? If so, when? If you're confident you'll find a new job soon, maybe you'll continue spending as usual, but are you really sure a new job will appear? The prudent thing to do is prepare for the worst. Maybe you have already put some money away for just such a situation, but that doesn't mean you should just use it up and worry about replenishing your savings later. Ask yourself this: can you adjust your lifestyle enough so if things get worse you'll still be okay? To put it another way, do you *need* to maintain your current spending habits, or do you merely *want* to?

In 1998, I was locked out of my job, along with 1,200 fellow union members. I had enough money put away that I was confident I could survive for the length of the lockout. All of us on the picket line thought the lockout would end quickly or the union would prevail in the courts and we'd all get back pay. As it turned out, the National Labor Relations Board sided with the company, and the lockout lasted eleven weeks. Even though I thought things wouldn't be too bad, I quickly made a decision to stop spending money. I don't mean I cut back a little; I spent almost nothing: no more dinners out, no movies, no new CDs, and no skiing, although I loved to ski and it was winter (which made walking the picket line all the more cold and miserable). During those eleven weeks, some nearly lost their houses, and I know of one person who even went bankrupt—but the only difference in my case was a difference of $4000 in my bank account. In spite of losing over $13,000 in pay, I still had virtually all my savings, was able to pay all my bills, and, in September of 2000, was even able to buy a vacation home with three apartments, two of which I rent during the summer.

I had lost my job (albeit briefly) and I had to make some difficult decisions. But this book isn't about how to handle worst-case scenarios; it's about how to do more with what you have now while being prepared for the worst. In that spirit, let us assume that nothing will change, and that you will not face a sudden loss of income; the fact remains that you want to be rich. By being rich, if it wasn't obvious already, I don't mean being able to retire at thirty, living out your remaining years on a yacht with young members of the opposite sex to cater to your every desire. I mean living comfortably and retiring early, or simply retiring with enough money that you don't have to worry about the future. To do this, you will have to make choices now to prepare for the future. ***Now is the time to think about the best course toward success.***

If the you-can-be-super-wealthy-too books I've read are true, everyone with access to a bookstore should be a millionaire now. The fact is there will always be poor people, the middle class, the rich, and the super rich. But—and this is a big but—you can do better. We can all do better, and I hope my words and the stories about other successful people will help you do so.

Although I said earlier that there are no rules and that I don't believe in lists, there is going to be some homework. You're going to have to actually apply some effort if you want to be rich. I know other books make it sound so easy, but I'm a realist, and the reality is that you have to do something if you want to get something in return. The first thing I want you to do is put yourself in a category. Financially speaking, are you a details person or do you wing it, thinking that as long as you have some money in the bank you're fine? What I'm getting at is this: do you balance your checkbook?

If you're the kind of person who knows where your money is coming from and going, you are ahead of the game. If you live paycheck to paycheck and don't keep really good records, you are in for a rude awakening. The first thing you have to do is start keeping track of every penny that passes through your hands. Keep a spreadsheet or use financial software such as Quicken or Microsoft Money. I use Quicken, but since they aren't paying me to say nice things about them, you can make your own choice. Besides, I've never used Microsoft Money. For all I know it's better.

The first thing I suggest is that you make a list of every account you have. By account, I mean things like savings accounts and checking accounts, but don't stop there! Add mortgages, credit cards (each individually), car loans, boat loans, and any other kind of loans out there. You're not done yet! Add brokerage accounts, money market accounts and any other accounts you can think of. If you don't have all of these things, don't worry; you will soon enough, and you'll have to keep track of them when you do.

The easiest types of accounts to manage are savings and checking accounts. There are really only two things to think about—what's going in and what's coming out. The obvious items going into these accounts are paychecks and any other income you might have including that little side business Uncle Sam might not know anything about.

Unlike a good diet, the secret to financial success (and it isn't a well kept secret) is to keep more than you spend. Of course when dieting you want to spend more calories than you take in but too many people do that with money and that's bad. Consider the advice in this book the anti-diet of money. With just a small amount of work, you'll be able to gain a great big potbelly of cash!

When you begin keeping track of your accounts, the opening balance should be what you currently have in that account. The best time to log this information is when you get your bank statement. When the statement arrives in the mail, open it up and see what the closing balance is. This will be your opening balance when you start using your tracking application. If you have $1,000 in checking and $5,000 in savings, that's the opening balance. You're done (for this month). If you have access to your bank account online then there's no need to wait till your paper statement arrives in the mail. Both Quicken and Microsoft Money will allow you to sync your account with your bank. I would not do this, however, if there is a fee for this service. ***Why pay for something you can easily do yourself?***

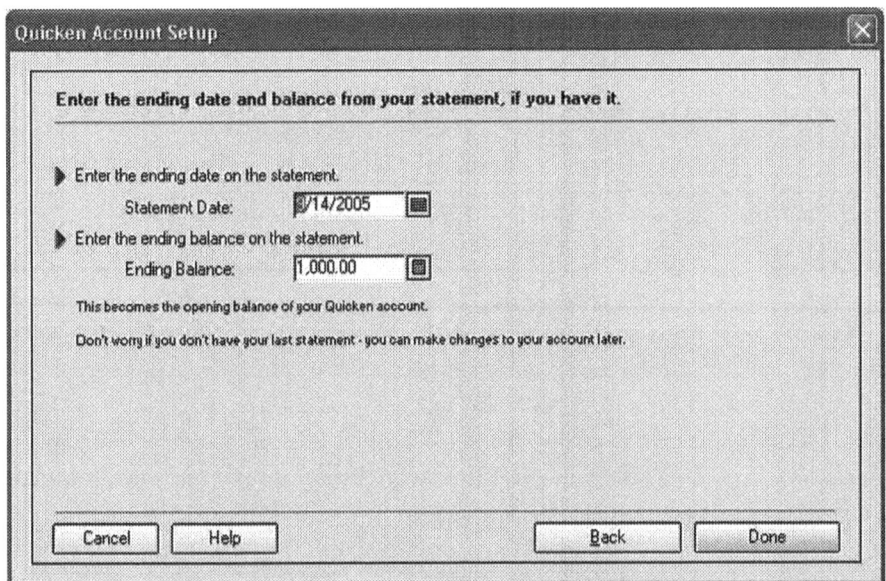

From this day forward, everything you do in those accounts will be documented. This means that when you take money from an ATM, you will enter it in your tracking application (spreadsheet or other software, such as Quicken). When you write a check, you must enter this into your tracking application as well; the duplicate (if you use them) or the cancelled check is not a sufficient record. The check registry, where you keep your balance, also isn't enough if you don't also enter it into your tracking application.

In order to have a complete understanding of your finances, however, you must also designate a category for each entry. For example, if you write a check for an oil change, enter this under the category "Auto Service" or something similar. Good records start with descriptive categories, so choose yours wisely.

| Rich's Checking | Register | Overview |

Delete   Find   Transfer   Reconcile   Write Checks   Set Up Online

Date/ △	Num	Payee/Category/Memo
9/14/2005		Opening Balance
		[Rich's Checking]
9/14/2005		Bill's Auto Service
		Auto:Service
9/14/2005	Num	Payee
		Category

You are now keeping good records, but you also have to check your work. This means when you receive your statement each month, you will need to reconcile (balance) the accounts to make sure you have what you think you have. This is also a good idea to ensure the bank hasn't made any mistakes. This might sound like a lot of work, but it isn't. You probably check your email at some point each evening; use this time to enter your financial information for the day as well. It won't take long to enter one or two transactions. Since you're now using your computer to keep track of your finances, you should pay your bills by the computer. It is a simple matter to enter everything into your tracking application right away. Do not do it later that day or the next day; do it right then—why do things twice?

"Now, Mr. Author," you may be asking, "is all of this really necessary?"

"Yes it is," I say, "and call me Rich."

So far, we have covered your basic savings and checking accounts, but the most important accounts to keep track of are credit cards. How you handle credit will determine how successful you are. Suze Orman, a highly respected financial advisor, author, and television host, whom I like and trust immensely (you should read her books too), said she could tell how much credit card debt someone had by how messy that person's car was. When my wife and I heard that, we looked at each other with horror. Our cars were a mess, with litter strewn throughout, CDs all over the place, and junk mail on the floor. Thankfully, we didn't have any credit card debt. And just because you keep your car clean doesn't mean you are debt free.

If you have a lot of credit card debt, address this issue first. Forget about cleaning your car; get to work reducing your debt! However, your goal is not simply to reduce your debt or get a better interest rate; your goal is to eliminate credit card debt completely. Does that mean you'll never have a balance again? No, but carrying a balance should be a last resort. You should only have a balance on your credit card when there is no other choice. The credit card companies would have a fit if they knew I was telling you this, so don't let them see this book. Credit card companies want you to have a balance, a big one, and they want you to pay the minimum. They aren't doing this because they want you to live the life you've always dreamed of; they're doing this so *they* can live the life you've always dreamed of.

If you have a lot of credit card debt, eliminating it isn't going to be easy or much fun, but I'm not here to make things easy; I'll leave that to the other books out there.

My father had a saying that he used when talking about the houses he owned: "I never bought a house I could afford," he'd say. If you've been paying attention so far, you have to ask yourself what I'm talking about. To this point, I've said it's important to live within your means, yet, in the very next breath, I seem to be telling you to do just the opposite. Well, I'm not. The point of that story is credit, or debt in general, isn't necessarily a bad thing, but you must choose wisely the type of debt you will carry. My father bought homes he couldn't "afford", and later sold them for more than he paid. If you could do that with the fancy car you really want but can't afford, I'd say go ahead and buy it, but cars don't appreciate, so stick with the Hyundai.

I know I keep getting diverted from the task at hand but hey all work and no tangents would make for a very boring book.

My advice to eliminate debt altogether seems to suggest that credit cards are things we should avoid altogether, doesn't it? The whole point of credit cards is that they enable us to buy things now and pay for them later, but you will always have to pay. Let's imagine that you have a credit card with an interest rate of 18 percent and you buy only one thing with it. Let's say you go out to dinner at a fancy, expensive restaurant, get a good bottle of wine, and really enjoy the evening together with your loved one. The bill comes and once you add your typical generous tip, the total comes to $225. I know it was expensive, but it was really good, and you really love your partner. Now, let's say you pay only $20 each month when the bill comes in. The chart below shows how long it will take you to pay for that dinner and how much it will cost once you add all the finance charges.

Month	Payment	Interest	Balance
1	$20	$0	$205
2	$20	$3.07	$188.07
3	$20	$2.82	$170.89
4	$20	$2.56	$153.45
5	$20	$2.30	$135.75
6	$20	$2.03	$117.78
7	$20	$1.76	$99.54
8	$20	$1.49	$81.03
9	$20	$1.21	$62.24
10	$20	$0.93	$43.17
11	$20	$0.65	$23.82
12	$20	$0.35	$4.17

The dinner that originally cost $225 really cost you over $244 and took over a year to pay off. The extra $19 or $20 dollars wasn't that much, especially since it was spread out over a year, but imagine the horror when you have a balance of $5,000 and pay only the minimum. Now take a good look at your current credit card bills. Even if you pay $100 a month, it will take you seven years and nine months to pay off a $5,000 balance with an 18 percent interest rate, and you'll have paid $4,311 in interest charges. That's a lot of money, almost as much as your original bill, and a long time to pay for things that you might not have needed in the first place.

"But my interest rate is much lower than that," you say? Well for a 14 percent rate, paying $100 a month, you'll pay $2,547 in interest over six years, and for a 9 percent rate, it will take you five years and three months to pay off your debt plus the $1,290 in interest. When you think about what you could have done with that money, these reduced figures don't sound much better, do they?

This chapter is about keeping records and losing credit card debt, and the two go hand in hand. If you don't keep good records, you just keep adding to your credit card debt without seeing exactly what you're spending the money on. I said earlier that you should have a record for each credit card you own. If you have three cards then you should have three accounts set up in your software tracking application.

When your statement comes and you sit down to pay the bill, take that opportunity to enter all the transactions you have made into your tracking application. "But it's all printed there already. Why do I have to do all that work again?"

Good question, you're really showing an interest in this and I appreciate it. The credit card statement is a static document that only gives you a snapshot of a brief moment in your spending life. By adding this information into the tracking application, you now have a living document that you can look back on to learn things about yourself. How much did I spend this year on dinner out versus last year? Did I spend more on car repairs than on entertainment? If you did then buy a new car, that's a wise decision if you ask me. Asking questions about your finances is a really good idea if you're serious about planning for the future. This is why it is so important to enter information into appropriate categories. What good does it do you to know that you spent $5,000 on stuff if you don't know what that stuff was? By the way, if you pay your bills online or check your statement online, you can probably download your credit card information, and your software application will remember the category from past purchases so you don't have to type it in each time.

I could spend page after page telling you the evils of credit card debt. There are entire books devoted to the subject, and there are entire companies devoted to helping you get out of it. If you're like the rest of the country, however, you might not listen and you might not even try the suggestions I'll make, after all, you aren't falling behind in your payments—are you?

In 2002, the average American had somewhere around $8,450 in credit card debt. That's a long way from zero, but zero is exactly what it should be. I said earlier that if you have three credit cards, you should keep track of them individually, but did you know the average person has eight credit cards? Probably, since chances are you're one of them. Perhaps you are one of the many people who carry a balance month to month and maybe you only pay the minimum, or maybe a bit more than the minimum, each month—good for you if that's the case—but if you can't pay your balance off tomorrow, then it's too high. It's that simple. Let me say that again. *If you can't pay off your credit cards right now, you have too much debt.* Some things bear repeating.

You know that eliminating your debt is the single most effective way to begin working toward financial independence. Without debt, you will be able to do so much more with what you have. You also know that I believe in common sense, that sometimes the most obvious answer is the right answer. This is true for getting rid of your debt as well.

Let's assume that you have three credit cards with a $2,000 balance on each one. The interest rates are 19 percent, 17 percent, and 9 percent. Which one would you pay off first? If you said anything other than the 19 percent one, you're wrong. The question of which to pay off first gets a bit more tricky when the balances are different. What if you had a $1,000 balance on the 19 percent card, $2,000 on the 17 percent card, and $5,000 on the 9 percent card? The answer remains the card with the highest interest rate. Was it obvious? Well it's pretty clear to me that paying as little interest as possible is the way to go, so get rid of the highest interest rate first. If you don't know what the rate is then shame on you! It's printed right on your statement!

The concept I'm about to give you is not my invention. If it isn't abundantly clear already, almost nothing in this book is. I've gotten this information from any number of sources and you can too. I'm no expert and, for the most part, neither are the experts. The idea of paying off the card with the highest interest first, working your way down, and adding your previous payments to each subsequent card is known as snowballing. Why? Just as a snowball rolling down a hill grows as it gathers more snow, so do your payments grow as you add them together.

Here's an easy example. Suppose that the minimum payment on each of your cards was $50. You would have to make at least those payments, so for the two lower-interest rate cards, that's exactly what you'll do. For the one you want to pay off the quickest (the highest interest rate card), you'll pay as much as you can afford to that card, let's say $200 a month ($200 + $50 + $50 = $300 for all three cards). You will continue at that rate until you have it paid off. Now you will attack the next highest interest rate (the 17 percent card), but you'll add the $200 you were paying for the high-interest-rate card to the minimum payment you were making to this card ($50) so that now you are paying a total of $250 to this card plus $50 to the other card for a total of $300. When that card is paid off, you'll apply that $250 to the minimum of the final card ($50) so that now you are paying a total of $300 to the last card. Throughout that example, the amount you were spending didn't change, but the power of that amount increased as your debt decreased. You will pay off the final card in no time at all and, viola, you will be debt free. How long this takes depends on how much debt you have and how well you control or even eliminate your new spending. If you intend to pay down debt aggressively, you should not be spending much at all.

I can go on spouting statistics to scare you away from abusing your credit cards, but I don't think this is necessary. You don't need to know that if you add up all the finance charges paid by Americans last year, you would get a total of $400 billion dollars. You already know what you have to do. Now all you need is discipline.

You also know that different kinds of debt require different ways of thinking. I've said that if you can't pay off your credit cards right now then you have too much debt, but the same can't be said for a mortgage. It is okay to have debt but credit cards have to be the worst kind of debt out there. So I'll say again; if you can't pay off your credit cards right now then you have too much debt. Don't live beyond your means!

Below is a sample of what typical credit card entries in your tracking application will look like.

Credit: Rich's Credit Card		Register	Overview				
Delete Find Transfer Reconcile Set Up Online				View ▾ Report ▾ Options ▾ How Do I?			
Date/△	Ref	Payee/Category/Memo		Charge	Clr	Payment	Balance
9/10/2005		Opening Balance [Rich's Credit Card]			R		0 00
9/11/2005		Shop Rite Groceries		125 00			125 00
9/12/2005		BP Auto:Fuel		50 00			175 00
9/12/2005		Joe's Restaurant Dining		65 00			240 00
9/12/2005	Ref	Payee Category	Memo	Charge		Payment	Enter Edit Split

If you've been following along and putting the advice in this book into practice, you now have several accounts set up in your tracking application. You're getting good at it, and maybe a bit bored, but keep going. This part is like cooking a fine meal: the more prep work you do, the easier the cooking will be later. In personal finance, the more accounts you add, the clearer your financial picture becomes and the more motivated you'll become to improve your situation. You are beginning to think of money in a real way, not just as some abstract thing you have a little bit of and always need more.

Before we move on to talking about what the heck to do with all this information, you have to ask yourself: *Is this something I can really do?* Are you going to be diligent about documenting every financial transaction you make? If the answer is no, put the book down and good luck, but if the answer is yes, then read on—you've taken the first step toward a life of fabulous riches (or something like that).

4

Need vs. Want

The big question we all have to ask ourselves when we're about to plunk down good money for something is this: Do I really need this, or do I just want it? In reality, it may not be that simple, but it is a good place to start. I definitely want a Ferrari but do I really need it? Yes! But I can't afford it, so that problem has been solved with almost no effort on my part! This getting rich thing really is easy.

I think the reason most people don't know where their money goes each month is that they don't think about it. It's that simple—they don't think about each purchase as if it's going to make a difference. They don't have a budget or an allowance, and they treat credit cards as free cash without consequences. They want to project success whether it's real or not! They want to keep up with the Jones's, and most of them don't even know anyone named Jones! The bottom line is, they don't exercise common sense.

It's not just keeping up with the next guy; it's keeping up with what the advertisers tell you. *The new Pentium chips are out and you still have the old one? What's wrong with you?* So you go out and buy the latest and fastest computer, even though you weren't actually having any problems with yours. After all, unless you're doing complicated 3D animations or mathematical equations for NASA, you don't need the fastest computer, but you buy it anyway. That's when you should be asking yourself, *What's wrong with me?*

I can't tell you how many times I've been jealous of friends because they have the newest or fastest or most cutting edge things and I don't. My cell phones have always been bigger than everyone else's, and they've lacked the "cool" features like cameras or internet capability. I was late to get a DVD player, because I just didn't need one. Although I have a newer television (made in 1999), I still have the one I had for fifteen years as my basement set and one I've had since 1997 in my bedroom. The reason I have two TVs from the late nineties is that in 1997, my girlfriend's (now wife) house burned down and we bought a TV to replace the one we lost. No matter how jealous I get of things other people have, I buy only the things that I need. As a matter of fact, in spite of the fact that I want a new laptop, I'm writing this on a 1996 Pentium 2 233 Mhz system (For all the non-geeks out there that's old). I'd love to have a new one but just don't need it.

Let me take a moment and be honest about that last paragraph. I'm actually writing this on a new laptop now. When I first wrote the paragraph above I was indeed using an old computer and had no intention of getting a new one. Then my wife broke the old one. She won't agree with that but that's my story and I'm sticking to it. Besides when she comes out with her tell-all book she can claim I actually broke it.

I just bought a new car, (no not a Ferrari) and after waiting almost four months, I finally took possession of it. It was a difficult wait but definitely worth it. When I met my wife (she wasn't my wife at the time) I was driving a four-year-old car and was ready for a new one, but I just wasn't sure if I could afford one. I had just left a full-time job for a temporary job that I hoped would become permanent. (It did.) Considering my situation, I didn't think buying a new car was such a good idea. For the next couple of years, we were busy with life, and a new car just wasn't a priority, although I never stopped looking at every new car I saw on the road or advertised on TV.

After getting married, affording a new car was no longer a problem, but we still didn't get one. We were both driving cars that were seven years old at the time. They worked and only occasionally needed minor repairs. Why buy new cars, I thought, when I take mass transit to work and my wife has a five-minute commute? Both cars worked and—this is important—***what we weren't spending on car payments we could save or invest***. We might have wanted new cars but we needed to save—for retirement, for a summer home, or just for a rainy day, because you know that spending money is what people do when it rains. Sure we had car payments when the cars were new, but once they were paid off, we had an extra $200 in my case and $300 in my wife's case per month with which we could do other things. Of course, a $200 car payment sounds good today, but twelve years ago that was a typical for my small car.

I still wanted a new car, however, and never tired of reminding my wife of this fact. She got tired of hearing it, but I was relentless. She was stronger. As the repairs got more serious, I thought my argument was gaining ground, but it would take almost two years of nagging on my part before she even agreed to go to a dealership with me.

When we finally did start looking, the cars were somewhat expensive ($30,000 to $40,000). The frugal part of me required that I look at more modestly priced cars, and so we also looked at cars that topped out at $25,000. What was our final decision? Well, knowing that we intended on keeping the new car for at least ten years, we went with the more expensive option. Oh yeah and my wife didn't want to have to hear that I liked other cars better—so my nagging did pay off after all.

There are some people who look at my wife and me and can't understand how we've been able to do so well. Sure we have good jobs that pay well, but so do they. We certainly don't consider ourselves rich, but that's how a lot of people think of us. We're a bit like a new singer who seems to come out of nowhere—people see only the *results* of the time and effort we put into our success, not the actual hard work.

I know many people who look rich. They drive expensive cars and dress well, but they struggle every week to make the bills. On the other hand, I look like a slob most of the time and not only don't I have a problem paying the bills, but I have plenty of money saved. The worse you look, the more you have. Okay so that's not really true—appearances are just that. Priorities are important, but knowing which ones to place before others is harder than it seems. I didn't believe this until I realized just how many people couldn't do it.

If you really want to be "rich," don't live beyond your means. I know I'm repeating myself, but this is important. You may be able to buy a new car every few years, but is that really the wisest use of your money? Keep the car a few years longer and use the saved car payments to work toward your dream, or put them toward the down payment of your next car. My brother has taken that concept to the next level. He's gone as far as opening a new savings account and depositing his previous car payment into that account each month. He then used these funds to put a down payment on his next car when he was ready. When he paid his bills, he treated this account just like any other, such as his mortgage or his electric bill. This insured that he would not cheat himself by spending this extra money on something he didn't really need. You've heard the concept of "paying yourself first." Well, think of this in the same terms.

But really, how many of us think about a major purchase like a car in the manner outlined above? Not many. If there is a purchase that you should give a lot of thought to, it is a car or a house. ***The more expensive an item is, the more you should think about its purchase.***

We all want a nice big house. We want to be as comfortable as we can. If I could afford a 5,000-square-foot house, I would get it. Do I need all that space, especially considering that I don't have any kids? No, but it would still be nice. I'd have a game room, a weight room, a bar, and any other amenities I could think of, because they would show that "I've made it." I want all these things, but do I need them?

When the time comes to purchase your first house (or second or third, for that matter) you need to know how much you can afford. A simple rule is 2.5 times your income; therefore, if you had an income of $50,000, you could afford a $125,000 mortgage. If you had $25,000 to use as a down payment on the house, you would be looking in the $150,000 range. Of course, in your search, you might find a house for $180,000 that you just fall in love with. In that case, what do you do? Maybe you can borrow the money from your parents or something, but I wouldn't recommend it. Unless the money is an interest free gift, you are still overextending yourself and that will not lead to increased wealth. Even if the money is a gift, you may yet be overextending yourself by buying a larger house with higher maintenance costs.

You shouldn't buy a bigger house than you need or one that you can't easily afford simply because you want it. Successful people didn't get that way by overextending themselves. Just because the mortgage company will give you a loan for a large amount of money doesn't mean that you can really afford it.

Considering the way real estate prices have increased lately, the "simple rule" I mentioned above will make it impossible to find a house within your means in many places throughout the country. Therefore, what's a perspective home buyer supposed to do? Well, that's what I mean when I say that you have to give a lot of thought to expensive purchases. Maybe your best bet is to rent for a while longer and see what happens to the prices. Rents have not increased as much as purchase prices, which indicates that home prices are overvalued, so there might be an opportunity there. For example, if it would cost you $3,000 a month in principal, interest, and expenses (insurance and taxes) to buy a house, but only $2,000 to rent a similar home, then maybe you should rent and save the difference. But the important point in that last sentence is to *save* the difference. That is how to increase your wealth.

Are you willing to sacrifice a bit now so that down the road you'll be that much better off? (I'll give you a hint: the answer should be yes). Rather than renting, as I suggested above, an equally good idea might be to look for a fixer-upper that costs less but which, with a bit of work, will give you a nice return when you decide to sell it. Maybe you're not a weekend warrior, but can you accept a slightly smaller house, with maybe one less bathroom, so that you aren't stretched too thin? Paying $10,000 less for a house might not make you rich, but it will give you the discipline that is necessary when other tough decisions come along, such as, *What will I have for lunch tomorrow?*

I stumbled across a website once that I highly recommend. I bookmarked it and use it to this day whenever I have a financial problem to work out. The site,

Hugh's Financial Calculators, has some really useful tools, as well as some that are more frivolous but no less important. You thought I was kidding about the lunch thing, didn't you? Hugh has a calculator that will tell you how much money you can save by bringing lunch from home rather than going out every day. If you smoke, there's a calculator to tell you how much money you'd save if you quit and, with cigarette prices what they are today, I think I've already shown that quitting is certainly worth considering.

Now is the time to start thinking in terms of need versus want. Think about what you're interested in buying and doing in the near future. Sit down, make a nice cup of tea or coffee, and make a list of all the things you want to get out of life. You want a new car? Fine, write that down. You want a new TV? A boat? A second home at the beach? In the country? You want to be able to send your kids to Harvard? You want to retire while you can still enjoy your life? You get the idea. Now, which items do you really *need*? Which ones do you want so bad that living without them will make you feel as if you are not successful? Now, what will you have to give up to get it? Life is a balancing act, and **the more balanced you are, the less you'll trip up**.

Sometimes you will need something someone else would not even want, but that is part of your uniqueness. Let me give you an example using a man I look up to, Ted Turner. Ted Turner needed to start CNN. He wanted it so badly that it became something he needed to do. This book is another example. I wanted to write a book for many reasons, but I kept telling myself I was crazy—who was I to tell you what you should do? But the idea just wouldn't go away, and I knew I had to do it if I wanted peace.

A word of caution before we continue. Each one of the suggestions below might be a good idea on its own, but if you try them all at once, there is a chance you will go a little too far and become a miser. I'm going to call this the miser clause. Don't become a cheapskate! No one can accuse me of being cheap or miserly, but many are amazed at what I'm able to do. Sure, my wife and I (mostly my wife) make a good living, but we also work very hard so we can have that extra bit of cushion.

I found the following chart on the *Motley Fool* website. Notice that if you add all the figures up (using the high end of the range), you'll be spending more than you earn. This is not uncommon, but your goal should be the low end, if possible (except for saving and investing, of course). The figures in parenthesis are what my wife and I spend on the items listed. This is a snapshot of a moment in time. I'm sure the numbers are different today from when I wrote this, that's why you need to keep this information current, to always know where you stand.

- Housing and utilities: 25–30 percent (13.67 percent combined primary residence and rental property)

- Food: 10–15 percent (1.36 percent)

- Vehicles: 10–15 percent (8.01 percent, includes car loans, fuel, insurance, registration and tolls)

- Insurance: 5 percent (1.74 percent, excluding primary residence which is included in housing)

- Saving and investing: 10–15 percent (25.58 percent)

- Entertainment: 5 percent (6.61 percent)

- Clothing: 5 percent (0.73 percent)

- Medical: 5 percent (0 percent)

- Childcare and education: 1–8 percent (0 percent)

- Gifts and charity: up to you

This exercise demonstrates that the information in this book is not just for you, it's also for me. Even those who are knowledgeable about their finances and do well saving and investing need to check themselves often. By doing this exercise, I learned that I can improve the categorization of my spending. You can see that I've only accounted for 57.7 percent of my income. Where did all the rest go? This shows the difficulty in keeping track of money. I'm good at it, but imagine how someone who doesn't keep track of their income and expenses will do. There are categories that aren't included on this list, such as the amount of taxes you pay and sometimes I simply don't know what category something belongs in and therefore log it under miscellaneous. Be careful with using miscellaneous as a category. It should be used sparingly if at all. I put every dollar I spend into a category in Quicken so when it's time to add them up, I simply ask Quicken how much I spent on each item. Doing this, Quicken tells me that I spent 66.59 percent of my income, which means I saved 33.41 percent. That is an incredibly high savings rate and is the reason we have amassed a high net worth at such a young age. The above list is a good start that gives you a quick and basic picture of your spending.

Here's how to come up with your own numbers for this chart. For this example, I'll use my numbers for housing and utilities. The formula looks like this:

$$\frac{(\text{mortgage} \times 12) + (1 \text{ year of utilities})}{\text{full year's income}} \quad \times \quad 100$$

For my income, I used the gross figure from Quicken, which represents any income I had, including salary, rental income, and gifts, among other things. I took my monthly mortgage payment and multiplied by twelve to come up with my full year's expenses. I then used Quicken to determine the amount of money I spent on utilities (cable, gas, electric, and water) the previous year. I added the mortgage and utility numbers and then divided by my income. This gave me a figure of 0.1367, which I then multiplied by 100 to get 13.67 percent. As you see, we could have afforded a larger, more expensive house, but we saw no reason to take on the additional expense for a house that was too big.

Once you have a complete understanding of where your money goes, you can move on and begin the real work toward financial independence and a future free from debt. What practical things can you do to begin working toward your goal? Well, I hope you've already taken the first step, to keep good records of your finances. Next, I would suggest a test. How do you know what you really need (as opposed to want) unless you try doing without it? I call this test "the three-month test," because I want you to *give up spending for three months*. That's right—three months without spending a dime. This, of course, does not include things like your mortgage or rent, utilities, groceries, gas for your car, or other necessities of modern life. I'm talking about discretionary spending.

Getting rich doesn't just involve earning lots of money. Actually, earning is only part of the equation. Discipline is learned, and the best way to learn is by doing, so start by curbing your spending. This won't be easy, but you can do it. The first time I took the three month test was when I, and the 1,200 other union members at my employer, were locked out for eleven weeks in late 1998 and early 1999. I had more incentive than you might, but this is a worthy exercise that will show you where your money is going, where you can cut back and just how much flexibility you really have.

I did this for the *first* time during the lockout, but I often retest myself to straighten out my priorities. Occasionally, I'll simply shut down my spending. I don't do it to see if I can, because I've already proven that, and I don't do it to see where my money is going, because I already know that. I do it to pull back and reevaluate my spending habits. Perhaps I'm going overboard on things I want while neglecting other things I need, or maybe I'm just not saving enough to meet my goals. Whatever the reason, occasionally doing a modified version of the three-month test helps to keep me grounded.

For your first time, however, this test means that you will give up all discretionary spending. This includes not going out to eat for three months. No take-out food or quick stops at McDonalds (or any other fast food establishment so I won't be accused of picking on the golden arches). No donuts, chips, smoothies, or other snacks (hey you might loose some weight too). Pack a lunch, otherwise you'll go hungry. Want to see a movie? You'd better hope it's on TV, because there will be no theaters for you. No buying CDs or DVDs. No magazines or books, and no coffee from your favorite boutique café. (You might be surprised at how much you save here.) No vacations or long weekends unless they won't cost you a thing.

This test will tell you if you are serious about your financial future. I'm tempted to allow you to modify the three-month test—cutting a month off or allowing for some discretionary spending—but I promise not to cop out if you don't. As I've said, many personal finance authors out there don't offer practical advice, and that's because they know the exercises are difficult. They simply want people to buy their books and attend their seminars. I want you to have something to work with. Sure I want to sell books, and collecting money for teaching seminars has its good points, but if I don't give you specific and useful guidance, then you wouldn't have a reason to buy the book or attend a seminar.

Three months without any discretionary spending might sound drastic, but I assure you that the money you save and the amount you will be able pay down on your credit card bills will astound you. The results of this test will open your eyes and provide you with the incentive to make serious progress toward financial independence. It will certainly show you that you can do more. You can save more, and you can control your spending habits. This will be hard work, but anything worth doing is going to take work. Are you serious or not? If you are, then three months is a small price to pay; after all, we're talking about the rest of your life.

5

Think, Talk, and Dream Money

There should be no secrets when it comes to money. Easier said than done when some people even lie to themselves. While I can understand maintaining financial privacy, you certainly should not hide the truth from your partner, your family, and especially yourself. You have to be honest with yourself and with those whom you share financial dependence.

Money is often a reason for divorce and unhappy marriages. All of my advice so far has been directed at you as an individual, but you aren't the only person in the world. What you do affects many other people, whether you know it or not. If you think only of yourself, you might be happier, but you might also be alone before you know it.

Everyone is different and we have to respect those differences while trying to work with one another. This is the psychological portion of the book, a sort of therapy session. I'm no Dr. Phil (thank God), but I still know that communication is vital to any relationship. Whether that relationship is business or personal, without communication, it just won't succeed.

If you are married or just seriously involved, perhaps living with someone, your finances are locked together whether you like it or not. This can be dangerous, because sometimes, as with your financial decisions, you might not choose a partner wisely and be stuck with someone you love completely but who just can't handle money. How many times have you heard someone complain that they don't have enough savings because their significant other just can't rein in their spending habits?

My wife has some experience with this. She went through a difficult financial period because of her ex-fiancé. He was horrible with money and used to spend it like he had it, as I like to say. Examples of their overindulging lifestyle included two personal watercraft, two brand new (and expensive) cars, as well as a large amount of credit card debt. They couldn't afford any of these things, but the things made them feel good. There was nothing my wife could do to stop this, she said.

If you've been following my advice, you know that I just can't let that go unchallenged. She knows it takes two to mamba (tango is so overused). She has to bear some of the responsibility for their troubles. If this little story sounds like your situation, put your foot down. Take the advice in this book and change your life now, while you still can.

If you're in a relationship, I assume that you love the other person and are willing, on occasion, to do things you don't want to in order to please him or her. You should be able to do the same with money. You should be willing to listen and forego some extravagances if your partner doesn't think they are wise. You should be able to discuss any financial topic, such as buying a new car or boat or funding a hobby, and come to an agreement without fighting or animosity. Easier said than done, isn't it?

You not only should be able to do this, but you must—it is the only way to insure that your goals match up and you aren't undermining your partner's future. Discussing finances and talking about your goals and where you stand is important to maintaining your progress. For those who are having problems with money, the prospect of talking about it probably sounds as appealing as talking about an open sore (sorry about that but it can be that bad for some people), but if there was ever a time to work together, this is it. My wife and I discuss our finances and goals quite often, even though it's not always a necessity. The fact that we do says a lot about how successful we are and will be in the future.

As I mentioned earlier, although I would *want* to buy a new car almost every year, I realize I don't *need* a new car every year, and my wife keeps a tight rein on me. We discussed buying a car often, until we finally made the move. In these discussions, we each presented our case and then made a decision based on the strength of our arguments. I knew it was hard to argue with the fact that we had two working vehicles and that spending money on a car we didn't really need would be a waste. I knew it was hard but I'd try any way because, in spite of being careful with money, I'm human, and have moments of weakness just like the next guy.

I know this bit of advice might sound a little strange, but communication with your partner or family isn't enough—you must also talk to yourself. I don't mean in the insane, yell and argue with yourself way, I mean you should be able to think about the pros and cons of every decision on your own before presenting them to anyone else. If this means talking to yourself, then do it. (Just don't let anyone see you.) Think of your discussions about finances as if they were a debate. You want to know what your opponent is going to say before they say it so you can respond intelligently. The best way to do that is to practice—have a fake discussion with yourself or bounce ideas off a trusted friend.

Talking to yourself or the saner sounding, preparing for a discussion, will help you make a more convincing argument or help you realize why your idea might not be so good after all. If you're honest with yourself, you can avoid major problems later with the person you discuss your finances with.

If you've begun keeping track of your finances, your discussions will be based less on emotion and more on the reality of your situation. Since you know where your money is coming from and where it's going, you can make more informed, intelligent decisions.

Let me give you an example of a discussion my wife and I had, in which I presented my case for buying a new truck earlier than we had planned. I felt we were spending too much on maintenance and that we were throwing money into a truck that would soon not be worth fixing. My wife said the repairs were still cheaper than what we would spend on car payments. If we hadn't been keeping track of our expenses, the discussion would have either ended there or devolved into an argument. We had facts, however.

I went over to the computer and showed her that so far that year we had spent $5,000 on repairs. My wife, however, pointed out that not all of them were for the truck. She was right, and I had to subtract the $500 we had spent on repairs to our other car. That still left us with $4,500 dollars in repairs. However, my wife then pointed out that the previous year we had only spent $500, so over the two years, we had spent only $2,500 a year.

I was losing this argument fast, and that's when she pulled out the big guns. She made me price out a new truck on *Autobytel.com* and figure out the financing. It turns out that if we had bought a new car in January, we would have spent over $5,000 on car payments. I had lost. We were better off paying for repairs, and it didn't matter if I pointed out that the time the truck was in the shop cost us in ways other than monetary; she was still right.

Later, though, her father had a triple bypass, and she was driving forty miles one way to visit him every day. One day, on the way to the hospital, the truck broke down. We were able to make it to the hospital but needed to be towed home. Luckily, our AAA membership included free towing up to a hundred miles, so it didn't cost us anything. The peace of mind that comes with having a dependable vehicle finally won her over to my side, and a couple of weeks later we had a new truck.

The point is, we discussed this important decision and didn't make any purchases until we were in agreement. Read on as if this book is meant just for you (it really is). *Think* about the ideas and advice. *Talk* about what you like and don't like in these pages. *Dream* about how much better you can do.

6

The Three Little Choices

You choose to live a certain way. You can decide that you will no longer live in debt, in fear of losing everything. You have a choice, and when you think about it, there are really only three possibilities (although different degrees of each): 1) you can live beyond your means, spending more than you make and digging yourself deeper into debt, 2) you can live at your means, paying all your bills, not going into debt, but not saving anything either, or 3) you can live below your means.

While there are indeed three options, the first two stink. How's that for a simple answer. If you want any kind of success out of life, the first two options are out of the question. You aren't going to have anything more than you already do if you go down either of those paths. You may have a nice car and live in a big house, but you won't have any assets, and when times turn tough, you'll wish you did.

I have a story for you about a woman who posted her financial plight on *The Motley Fool* website's message board. The message board topic was "Living below Your Means" (on the "Managing Your Finances" board). Her story is not rare and the figures are not atypical. This woman told readers how she had wracked up over $65,000 in debt before deciding enough was enough. Reality struck and it hurt.

She then described how she was able to turn her life around. She put many of the things in this book to practice, and she figured it out on her own. She didn't need this book, because, as I said before, it doesn't take a genius to figure out that spending more money than you make is a stupid thing to do. I'm not re-inventing the wheel, I'm telling you things anyone could figure out if they would just be honest with themselves.

Without thinking, just answer this question: Do you live beyond your means? You know the answer. If you have a nice car that costs you an arm and a leg but makes you feel good, the answer is probably yes. If you live in a house that is too big to maintain, I bet the answer is yes.

Saving for retirement or having money in the bank doesn't mean that you aren't also in debt. I've said it before and I'll say it again: if you can't pay off your credit cards today and still have savings in case of an emergency, you have too much debt. You might fully fund your 401(k) or might even have a six-to eight-month emergency fund, but that won't always be enough. I call this living at your means, because I think that to truly get ahead, you have to live further below your means. This is tricky, because it requires balance. You don't want to focus so much on living below your means that you deprive yourself of any pleasure in life. As I said before, you do not want to become a miser.

Life isn't fair, but that's just the way it is—you can either complain about it or do something. I'd rather do something. It is much easier for someone who makes a lot of money to live below their means. The real test is whether you can do it while not making a lot of money.

Don't ever question the value of living below your means. Every year there are stories in the press that demonstrate the power of living simply and saving more than you spend. A recent example is that of a schoolteacher, who never made more than $28,000 a year but who left 2.1 million dollars to the school when he died so they could set up a scholarship. You can be sure that he lived a life I could never live. He bought expired meat to save money, something I think is just too drastic. The fact that he could amass such a fortune, however, is evidence of a couple of things. First, saving makes a difference and, second, compounding is a powerful tool.

In stark contrast to our teacher above, do you know someone who doesn't make that much money but drives a BMW? Are you that person? Do you, or someone you know, shop at expensive stores like Saks or Nordstrom or even Macy's? Have you ever shopped at discount stores such as TJ Maxx, Marshall's, Sears, or even Costco? Well if you have, then good for you, but be careful—just because something is cheaper doesn't mean that you need it. If you're the type of person who says, "Hey I'm at Costco, so I'll buy fifty pounds of lobster," you don't get the concept of discount shopping.

Since I mentioned shopping and getting a good deal, you should know that I think supermarkets and other big chain stores have a great scam going, and we're all the victims. I'm talking about the evil "club card" or whatever they call those store cards that you need to save big at the register. Why are they a scam, you ask? Well I'll explain, and I'm glad you're asking so many questions. This shows you're willing to learn.

Once upon a time, companies would put an item on sale, and you would go to the store and buy that item cheaper than you did last time you were there. You didn't have to do anything but go to the store and buy the item. The store wasn't losing any money; they were simply passing their savings on to you. Someone came up with a great idea, however, and you and I were on the losing end. "What if we could keep the extra money from the sale price and not pass it along to the customer?" they asked. That's when the club card was born. If you wanted the sale price, you needed the club card. If you didn't have the card, you paid the full price even though the store was paying much less this time.

I was always against those cards, because I believe if an item is on sale, it ought to be on sale for everyone. The problem with my thinking, my refusal to get the card, was that I was paying much more than I needed to. This is when I realized that every decision is a financial decision. If you start thinking about everything you do in terms of money, you can easily begin to live below your means, keeping more money for important things, such as retiring early, starting your own business, or just treating yourself to things that will truly make you happy, such as a great vacation every year.

We can all dream of the things we want—the new cars, the big house, the fabulous vacations—but we know that all of it comes with a price. Although there are no set rules for becoming rich, common sense still matters. I can't stress this enough and will not get tired of reminding you. If I became rich by spending half my paycheck each week on lottery tickets and finally win, that doesn't mean you should too. The chances are you won't win. That's common sense.

Speaking of lotteries, I think they're evil, not in the biblical sense just in the waste of time and money sense. Do I play? Once in a while I might. The last time I played the lottery was well over a year ago, possibly two. My wife, on the other hand, does play occasionally, but it doesn't make a dent in our income. I still don't like the fact that she plays, but it's her money. She's probably spent only $50 or $100 the whole year. What drives me nuts is the people who spend $10, $20, $30, or more dollars a week. If that's you, stop! Stop right now! By playing the lottery, you're saying, "Hey, I'm not good enough to do this on my own—I need a miracle," but you don't—you need discipline. A dollar and a dream, the slogan goes, but it's more like a dollar and a pipe dream.

There's a reason state-run lotteries have been described as the "idiot tax." State-run lotteries are big business, and they take in incredible amounts of money. In New Jersey, where I live, the combined take from all the lotteries is $2,068,506,868 (2001-2002 fiscal year). The population of New Jersey in 2000 was 8,414,350 people, meaning that every man, woman, and child in the state spent $245.83. Now, we know that children can't play the lottery, so that means some of you Jerseyans are spending a lot more than $245.83.

I can't stress enough that lotteries and other forms of gambling are a colossal waste of your time and resources. You must use your financial resources wisely, and taking a chance on something with odds like 150 million to 1 is simply not sensible. People do win big lotteries, but everyone who plays and hasn't won is a loser.

If you still think it's a good idea to play the lottery, then let's do a little test (you can tell I like tests). Write down every penny you spend on lottery tickets for one year. At the end of the year, add up all the money you spent and subtract your winnings. If your winnings were higher than the cost of your tickets, then fine, continue dreaming, but if you spent more than you won, give it up! It's important to do this today, not right after a big win.

Part of having financial discipline is weighing the cost and benefit of every decision. Unfortunately a lot of this is subjective. While we were able to come up with a test to determine if playing the lottery is reasonable, no such test exists for most spending. You have to decide if an expense is worth it or not. For instance, how often do you go out to dinner? Once a week? Twice a week? At some point, you have to ask yourself, *Is this really worth it?*

In 2002, my wife and I spent about $2,400 on dinners out (right around the national average). Based on our income, this is reasonable for us, but there are many things we could have done with that money. That's about four or five car payments now that we've buckled under the pressure and bought a new car. With $2,400, you can afford a really nice vacation or a new computer (if you really need one). The point is that you have to really think about your purchases before you make them and not just figure everything out at the end of the year. **Curb your impulses.** I have to stop again and warn you. I have to keep reminding you, because I have to keep reminding myself that too much of a good thing isn't really that good. You can get carried away and become a cheap bastard, and that's never a good thing.

Take care not to carry your cost-cutting practices too far, however. The *Tightwad Gazette* was a newsletter that gave great tips on how to squeeze the most out of each dollar you spend. But some of their tips cross the line into miserly existence. One example was reusing vacuum cleaner bags by slicing them open, dumping the dirt into the trash, sewing the bag up, and using it again. In this case, and in others, you have to ask yourself if the time you've spent is worth the pennies you've saved.

Thinking about everything in financial terms, however, is still a good idea. I thought about the vacuum cleaner trick for a second but didn't think it was worth it. Someone else might think it was a great idea, however, and if it works for them, that's great; I couldn't recommend it more.

When it comes to finances, you have to think of every option. When you buy a car, for example, don't settle for the low interest rate at the dealer; look for other options that aren't necessarily out in the open. When my wife and I were ready to pay for our new car, we were fortunate enough to have several options because of our good planning and fiscal restraint. We could either finance through the dealership at a rate of about 4 percent, get a home equity loan at about 5.5 percent (with an after-tax equivalent of 3.9 percent), or just pay cash. Because we were willing to live with older cars for some time and hadn't spent the extra money we had been saving without car payments, we had enough cash to buy the car outright and still have savings in the case of any costly unforeseen events.

The important concept to take away from this little story is this: if you can avoid interest, do it. The option of a home equity loan was still there for us, but why should we use it before we needed it? Why pay the bank for something we really didn't need? If we found that we were beginning to struggle, or if an urgent financial need arose, we could take a smaller loan until we were able to get back to normal. This is not to say that paying cash for a new car should be your goal. The point is that when you are financially intelligent and have extra cash on hand, you will have many more opportunities than most people.

In the example above, I mentioned a home equity loan. This is another way the rich get richer. They think about all aspects of money, looking beyond the surface and getting deeper into the truth behind the numbers. If you had the option of a new car loan at 5 percent interest or a home equity loan at 5.5 percent interest, which one would you choose? Well, the quick and easy answer might be the lower interest rate car loan. But every penny you spend will be lost, because the interest is not tax deductible. If you use your home equity loan at 5.5 percent, you can deduct the interest (in most cases) and save a bit of money.

Assuming you are in the 28 percent tax bracket, the 5.5 percent home equity loan will actually only be 3.9 percent, because you will be able to deduct the interest from your income. However, there are other matters to consider. You don't want to get a home equity loan just because you're going to save a few percentage points. Remember, this is your home we're talking about, and if you don't have to add to your debt on this asset, don't. But if you can easily afford it and believe it is the better option, go for it.

From the moment you wake up to the moment you go to sleep, money is a part of your life. If you eat breakfast—and you should, since it's the most important meal of the day—you have an opportunity to save money or waste it. If you buy pre-packaged waffles, for example, you'll be spending a whole lot more than if you make the waffles yourself. You might not have the time, however, but that is a decision that might save you money. You might stop at a local store on your way to work and buy a newspaper and coffee, but what if you subscribed to the paper instead and made your own coffee? That's how you save money; that's how you live below your means.

How far below your means you live is up to you. Some people can do without a lot more than others, but the fact is that living below your means is the only real way to get ahead. Looking at the things I have, you might think I'm just another one of these people who project success through appearances, yet I still live below my means. The more you have the easier it is. Bill Gates can live below his means and still spend hundreds of millions of dollars. The hard, but necessary, part is doing more with less. The choice is yours.

7

Hard Work

I had run out of milk one day and went to the local convenience store to get more since I wasn't about to skip breakfast. Breakfast is the most important meal of the day, right? I noticed that the store was owned by people of middle-eastern descent. Now I'm not saying this to be racist, or xenophobic, but it's a fact that a good number of convenience stores and other small shops are owned by people of Asian or middle-eastern descent. I always admire those who come from other countries looking for prosperity and start up their own businesses, despite their meager funds on arrival. Imagine if you moved to a foreign country and had to start from scratch. How would you do?

How do people who start with so little manage to do so much? The answer is simple, but most Americans, born into luxury and affluence, aren't willing to do what it takes. ***The people who can make something out of seemingly nothing are those who are willing to sacrifice to get what they want***. How many of you still live with your parents or, more accurately, how many of you have parents who still live with you? Many who come to this country are willing to do whatever it takes to make a better life for themselves. They will live in a small apartment or a house with several families so they can eventually afford their own business. They will work long hours seven days a week, sometimes even working two jobs.

I have seen this firsthand. When I was in high school and college, I spent summers at my parents' vacation home at the Jersey Shore. I worked in order to earn spending money, which I would quickly blow. I started as a dishwasher and moved up to cook. The local chamber of commerce recruited foreign students attending college in the U.S. to work at local businesses, and several of them worked with me at the restaurant.

These students were not like my college friends—they didn't have an endless supply of money to buy books or pay for tuition. In fact, some of the guys from the poorer countries were even sending money home to help their families. They were not spending the money they earned washing dishes; they were saving it. What was spending money to me and my friends meant a better life for them and their families.

One summer, two of these students were working with us. Paul was from Indonesia and a man whose name escapes me was from Kenya. Paul had a child back in Indonesia and was sending money back home to care for his family. Paul would work from 4 P.M. until 11:30 P.M. at the restaurant, go home, sleep, and get up early the next morning to be at his other job at McDonald's, where he worked from 6 A.M. to 3 P.M. Both jobs were six days a week. Although the gentleman from Kenya seemed to come from a more well off family, he too worked two jobs, something almost none of the Americans did, because their real goal was to party all night and spend their days on the beach.

This is the problem with us Americans. We want it all, but we aren't willing to work hard to get it. When my wife and I bought our vacation rental property in the same shore town where I spent my childhood, some of the tenants who had known the previous owners for many years were skeptical that we would be willing to work as hard as they had to maintain the apartments. Harry, the previous owner, immediately stood up for us, saying we were "hard workers" who had put a lot of effort into getting to the point where we could afford that property. I didn't see it that way, but I appreciated that Harry had stuck up for us.

I always thought of myself as a lazy person. "Why do today what you can put off indefinitely?" was my motto. The truth was a bit different, but I couldn't see it. Yes, I was lazy when it came to things like washing my car or cleaning my own house, but when money was involved, when my laziness would cost me money or cause me to miss an opportunity, I always found motivation. I did work hard, and I wanted to do the best I could at whatever job I had. I knew I was a good worker, but not necessarily a hard worker.

Once we bought the rental property, however, my wife didn't recognize me. I was always sweeping, taking out the trash, pulling weeds or cleaning for our guests. I still don't do that kind of stuff at home, but since rent was involved I was relentless. My wife and I each have good-paying full-time jobs that sometimes require us to work long hours. We also clean our rental apartments and maintain our property each weekend between renters. In the off-season, we usually remodel a room or more in order to give our tenants the best value we can. That means we spend most weekends working on some aspect of the house. We also designed and maintain a website for the apartments. And now my wife makes decorative soaps, which is turning into quite a good side-business. Do we work hard? Yes we do.

Our hard work is not a conscious decision. We didn't wake up one day and say, "Let's work hard today." We simply know that if we want to get ahead, we have to put some effort into it. Many people don't seem to understand this. Or maybe they just don't want to get it. They want the quick fix, the easy way, but it doesn't exist.

My dream has been, and still is, to open my own restaurant. I may not be a chef, but it has been a dream of mine for a very long time. I had an uncle who twice opened successful restaurants only to see them fail. We sometimes jokingly called him the original riches to rags story. If I tell anyone of this fantasy of mine, I almost always get the same answer: "Do you know how much work that is?" They're right—it is a tremendous amount of work, and wild riches are not guaranteed. More often than not, even if you are successful, you won't be rich. Not in the millionaire sports star or actor sense of the word.

The reaction I get from people indicates to me *they* aren't willing to put that kind of work into something that involves a great deal of risk. In other words, they aren't willing to sacrifice now to get more later. They would rather believe the get-rich-quick schemes on the infomercials they see. If you aren't willing to take a risk, however, how do you expect to get what you want? My desire to open a restaurant is just a want right now, but the idea will continue to develop, and one day it will become a need. I won't be able to tell myself "no" anymore, and at that point I will need to take the plunge and give it a try. That's when an idea totally consumes you, so much that you can't ignore it any more. You simply can't say your desire for some unnecessary item such as a plasma screen TV is the same. If you try, I'll tell you you're crazy. It's just not the same thing.

So far in this book, all I've given you is some discipline to keep better records and prioritize what it is you really want. If you've decided to take the three-month test, you've at least shown a desire to change your life. So then, how do you really get rich? I do have the answer, but it might not be what you want to hear.

The old saying "You'll never get rich working for somebody else" is absolutely false. I know this goes against everything you've heard, but it's not the end of the world. There are plenty of "Microsoft Millionaires" out there who worked for someone else and are very rich today. There are executives at large companies who work for someone else and are filthy rich. However, not all of us are going to be top executives. Not all of us are going to work for the next great company, receiving stock options that will make us millionaires many times over. Then there are some people who just made really good decisions and chose professions that make more money than others. Lawyers are a good example, but they have to deal with the fact that most people think they're scum. If you can get past that, and you're good, then being a lawyer (and working for someone else) can be very lucrative.

But still, working for someone else is not what we value here in America. What we value is the self-made millionaire, the guy who took the risk and went out on his own and now has a successful business working for himself. The internet revolution is full of people like that. Mark Cuban founded *Broadcast.com* and eventually sold it for billions to Yahoo! The downside to going it alone is that it's just as easy—no, definitely easier—to fail this way than to succeed. The greater the risk, the greater the reward or failure—but don't forget the failure. Of course, the other problem is that while it looks like they're working for themselves, they're not.

A restaurant owner doesn't work for himself; he works for the dinner guests who grace his establishment each evening. The heating contractor doesn't work for himself; he works for his clients, who could just as easily call the next guy. The CEO of company X isn't the boss; the shareholders and board of directors are, and although it takes a lot, they can fire him. No matter how hard you try to be independent, there's always someone to answer to.

We know this is true, yet we still hear people tell us that working for a corporation is a dead end. Back to Robert Kiyosaki and his rich dad's advice. He describes working for a corporation as being a "docile cow ready for milking." Serving two masters is what he says working for someone else is. You work for a paycheck and you work for the government (taxes). And he's right to some extent. The most successful people don't rely on only one source of income. But being rich and working for a paycheck aren't mutually exclusive.

Imagine if every lawyer (people who make a good living) started his or her own firm. They wouldn't be able to hire any other attorneys, because they would all be starting their own firms. Imagine if every bank teller started his or her own bank, every stock boy his own supermarket, there would be plenty of banks and supermarkets but no one to work in them. Not everyone can own their own business. It's not enough to say that the difference between rich and poor is that the rich work for themselves and the poor work for someone else. It's just not that simple, and if you want to be rich, you have to realize that if you think simply, you won't get anywhere.

Remember what we discussed earlier? (well ok so we didn't actually speak but humor me). You have to be willing to sacrifice now for more later. Take Jake Burton as an example.

"Who is Jake Burton?" you ask.

Jake is the founder and CEO of Burton Snowboards and is worth a lot of money—he is rich. What surprised me about the people who have made their millions is they were at it much longer than I thought. Jake started experimenting with snowboards back in the late 1970s! He quit his job and started making snowboards in his apartment in December of 1977. It wasn't until 1984 that Burton got his first real big break, when Stratton Ski Resort in Vermont was the first slope to allow snowboarders onto the mountain. Between 1977 and 1984, seven years, Jake made snowboards, but no one had any place to use them. People improvised and found places on their own, but that is some obstacle to overcome, and yet he stayed with it.

Jake Burton had an advantage that many people don't have when they decide to start a business: he had $120,000 to invest. You would think this would be enough, but he admits not being very smart about the whole business thing at the time, and he lost it all, even going into debt before turning things around.

Jake Burton was successful because he was persistent and willing to sacrifice. He went from having very little to having more than most people in the world. But for every Jake Burton there are thousands of people who are not rich but successful enough to have great lives. Take my father for instance. My father worked very hard all his life. He is not rich by any stretch of the imagination, but he was a success (a great dad) and is enjoying his life thanks to the sacrifice he made. My mother also deserves a lot of the credit for this, because she applied a lot of the discipline that I spoke of earlier. She improved my father's concept of bookkeeping at his heating business, taking receipts stuffed in a paper bag and creating an actual filing system. My father could fix or install any heating system, while my mother could organize and run the office—it was a perfect combination.

Although my dad is not my biological father, the distinction has never mattered to me. I've mentioned the popular book *Rich Dad, Poor Dad*, by Robert Kiyosaki, several times. The point of Robert's book is that he learned more about finances from his friend's father, the rich dad, than he did from his biological father, his poor dad. Well, I too had a rich dad, my stepfather, and a poor dad, my biological father.

My "rich dad" gave me very little direct advice about money, but his example was enough. I think this is evidence that the lessons are out there if you just open your eyes and look for them. I met my father when I was five (that sounds weird doesn't it), when he and my mother were just dating. I knew he was a fireman and was excited about meeting a real fireman. When he arrived, I greeted him at the door and asked him how many fires he had put out that day.

"None," he said.

"Then why are your hands so dirty," I replied. I didn't miss a trick back then, and besides, what kind of guy who didn't put out fires had dirty hands?

"I worked at my other job, and my hands get really dirty there," he said, and that was fine for me.

This exchange was completely lost on a five-year-old, but the important part was that he worked two jobs. His first job was as a fire captain in the busiest fire department in NJ. His other job was as a heating contractor. He installed and repaired people's heating systems in their homes and, occasionally, larger jobs such as apartment complexes.

This is sacrifice. He worked two full-time jobs for thirty years, and in 1980 when he and my mother married, he retired from the fire department and devoted himself completely to his heating business, which eventually expanded beyond the home market to a commercial clientele. He now only had one job, but he still put in more hours than most people do at their jobs. He provided for his children not only by putting a roof over their heads and giving them all the benefits he could, but most of us worked for him as well.

You'll never see his name on the *Forbes* list of the 400 richest people but he did all right. Would he like to have done better? Yes, we all would, but unfortunately many of us trade instant gratification (the big house, the fancy car) for future wealth. There are many people out there who would like to be as successful as my father. They all have the same chances he had, but the difference is that my father was willing to work for it.

I am not encouraging you to go out and get another job or work all the overtime you can. I just want to show that if you're willing to work hard, there is a reward. But, as in the story of Jake Burton, there is some luck involved too. I read somewhere that luck is when preparation meets opportunity. Jake saw the opportunity in a new product and was there from the beginning. He had the right idea at the right time, and in spite of his lack of business skill in the beginning, was able to make it work.

We know it takes effort, yet we hear things like: "Don't work for money; let your money work for you." I've heard that a thousand times. It's a common phrase that a friend of mine used to say, and I've seen in print, but it doesn't tell me much. It's a nice thought, but how can I actually use that principle to become rich? Does that mean I can retire and just let my money do the work? I'm afraid not. In the movie *It's a Wonderful Life*, the main character, George Bailey, owns a savings and loan during the Depression. There's a run on the bank, and George convinces everyone to take only what they need rather than pull all their money out. At the end of the day, George and his savings and loan are left with two one-dollar bills. George holds them up and says, "Let's put these in the safe—maybe they'll make babies." Money doesn't work for you—it's paper! No matter where your money is invested, it still takes time and energy to make sure you get the best returns possible.

Two quick examples of money not being able to work for you without your input. If you invest in stocks and bonds, you must be vigilant in order to make sure those investments are performing up to your expectations. You simply can't let the money take care of itself. If you own a business, you must constantly innovate and make improvements to keep your customers happy. It's not enough to buy or start a business and think the revenue will grow without effort.

I know I sound like I'm picking on Robert Kiyosaki and his *Rich Dad, Poor Dad* book, but I'm not. The book was much better than I had expected. I've read reviews that skewered him and the book as just another real-estate investment scam book written by a liar. In the book, Robert says, "Sometimes, I even start companies and take them public," but he can't point to one company that he has done that with. In spite of the negative reviews, I read the book and found it to be a decent motivator. I truly didn't expect this at all.

What did I like most about his book? It gets the reader to think about finances. This is really what people need, a kick in the behind to wake them up and make them begin thinking about money rather than complaining that they don't have enough. That's an important aspect of my book as well when you get down to it. One review I read, however, doesn't believe this argument for a second.

John T. Reed is a real estate investor who has made it his mission to debunk real estate "gurus" such as Robert Kiyosaki. In Mr. Reed's extensive review of *Rich Dad, Poor Dad*, (found at www.johntreed.com/kiyosaki.html) he takes some time to address the "it made me think about my finances" argument.

Mr. Reed writes,

> I think these 'made me think about finances' comments are inarticulate at best and dishonest at worst. What is really going on is a lot of people are schlepping along doing a half-ass job of managing the financial aspects of their lives. *Rich Dad Poor Dad* slaps them up side the head and tells them to clean up their acts. That's good, but the book goes on to deliver a pack of lies that make getting rich seem much easier than it really is and make education sound much less valuable than it really is. Basically, people want to get rich quick without effort. Kiyosaki is just the latest in a long line of con men who pander to that naive longing.

Clear and to the point, that's why I like Mr. Reed's reviews. He doesn't dismiss the argument about books like this helping the reader to think differently, he simply says that it's not enough if it isn't followed with good advice. While I agree that much of the information in *Rich Dad, Poor Dad* is not only wrong but dangerous, I did find some of it useful. The key is being able to toss the junk and keep the bits of good information. It would be much better if all the information was useful. I hope that my addition to the personal finance arena will meet that goal.

One of the problems with *Rich Dad, Poor Dad* is that while Robert says one thing, his examples demonstrate the opposite. Mr. Kiyosaki tells the story of how he got started investing in real estate. This story proves my point, that hard work is the path to success and wealth, more than his, that the rich let their money work for them. According to Mr. Kiyosaki, after college and after serving in the Marine Corps, he worked at Xerox apparently selling copy machines in Hawaii. In order to grow his own business, he says he became a "better employee." "I wanted out of the trap of being an employee so badly," he writes, "that I worked harder, not less." This is exactly my point. Working for the corporation wasn't the end; it was a means to the end.

Although I only get a paycheck from one employer, I feel I have two or three jobs. I work for a major corporation, but I also work for my vacation rental property and for my wife's soap company. Similarly, my wife has many jobs but just one paycheck. She gets paid by a different major corporation, but also works for our vacation rental property as well as her soap company. Will we always work at our "regular" jobs? I don't know yet, but I can tell you that if we do, we will do it because we want to rather than because we have to.

8

An Easier Way

Hard work and sacrifice are fine, but it seems like there has to be a quicker way to riches. You're right! There is an easier way, and I'm here to tell you what it is! Write this book. Yes, that's all there is to it. Look at me. I never wrote a book in my life before this one, and here you are reading my words. If I have sold a lot of these, I'm probably doing fairly well, so why can't you. Take this little test to see if you have the skills I had to write this book.

Are you one of the super rich? Good, because neither am I.

Are you a financial professional? Me neither.

Have you had any training as a writer or been published? Not me.

Do you speak English? That helps.

Do you want to get rich quick? It's that easy.

Of course, there are other ways to get rich if the prospect of sitting at a computer for days, weeks, and months doesn't appeal to you. **There are examples of success all around you**. You just have to say, "Hey I can do that too" and then get cracking.

Bored one early Sunday morning, I turned the television on. There were plenty of get-rich-quick infomercials on (and we'll deal with them in more detail later), but I also noticed while switching channels that there was a lot of religious programming out there, and that's when the light bulb went on. Why not become a televangelist! Have you seen the suits these guys wear? The amount of money they spend building their great chapels is probably a fraction of what they take home. The best part is that all you have to do is offer people a little hope and they'll just give you money. Sounds a lot like the get-rich-quick infomercials. And the best part is, you don't have to pay taxes.

I remember seeing a televangelist trying to explain away the bad press he had been getting over his wealthy lifestyle. He was going on about how the press had described his home as a mansion. "Some people would call it a mansion, but…"

he protested. Yeah if "some" means 99 percent of the U.S. population—you know, those of us who make less than a few million a year.

The best part is, just as in some financial books out there, you don't even have to say very much of substance. "Have faith" or "believe" or "amen" will do. What you do need is charisma, access to a television camera, and a station in need of programming to broadcast it, but hey, I never said any of this was going to be *that* easy. This is certainly easier than working two jobs or taking the risk of starting your own business, isn't it?

If you're worried about dishonesty, don't. What's the worst that can happen? A little tax problem? A little guilt about taking an elderly woman's only means of support? Judgment? That's a long way off. And who knows? By then, you might have done some good things in life.

As for the infomercials I skipped over, I flipped back to them and learned that I could buy a house for just $500 and sell it for $64,000. Yup, and that's not all—I could do this over and over again. I know it's true, because I saw real people who had applied these very real-estate secrets, which they would reveal to me for only $60. Too bad I had to get up off the couch to get the phone, or I would have ordered!

If actually buying the property and then selling it was too much work, there was another infomercial that said all I had to do was find property for sale, list it with them, and collect a check. Sure, the profits weren't as high as the ones in the previous example, but the work was so much less stressful. I could literally find a property, log on to their website, list the property, and then walk to my mailbox and collect a check—apparently someone out there was just waiting to put the check in my mailbox. Why people work for a living I'll never figure out. All we have to do is buy and sell real estate.

Of course, real estate is not for everyone, but don't despair. Maybe cars are your thing. Well you're in luck, because you can do the same thing with cars as you can with real estate. All you have to do is pay $60 and put the secrets to work! Imagine how rich I would be if I applied my principles of hard work and bought all the products I saw on these infomercials in just one day. I could place small classified ads in newspapers no one reads, buy and sell houses, cars, and who knows what else, and be the next Bill Gates.

Maybe you could become an artist. If you can draw a turtle, why can't you be the next Picasso or Peter Max. Of course, there's no promise of riches, but I was in a television commercial feeding frenzy and saw opportunity everywhere. What kind of author would I be if I didn't share these jewels of knowledge with you?

Speaking of real estate, before I leave that topic, there is one thing you have to remember about becoming rich. Don't limit yourself! This is immensely important. You can make only so much money buying and selling real estate that people have easy access to. You can make real money by selling something no one else in the world has. I'm talking about the moon, baby.

This book isn't just about me. I've said it before and I'll say it again. There are people out there much smarter and much, much richer than I am. Dennis Hope is one of them, and I'll tell you his secret for free, it's my gift for your purchase of this book. Mr. Hope sells property on the moon and has gotten rich doing it. I'm not kidding at all.

If you put this book down right now and go to www.lunarembassy.com, you'll find one-acre lots on the moon for just $19.95. I'm not so sure you'll be able to sell it for a $64,000 profit right away, but when people start emigrating to the moon, you'll have a head start.

I know this sounds like a scam, but many people have bought into it, and it sure seems legitimate. But how can someone who has never been to the moon own it? How can anyone own the moon? These are all good questions, and the answer is loopholes. Loopholes are probably the most powerful tool there is for the aspiring rich. Laws? What are laws but means to a loophole?

You see, Mr. Hope found that after the United States sent men to the moon, the United Nations signed a treaty banning any government from owning any part of space, including the moon, planets, or anything else. The loophole is that Mr. Hope is not a government—he's a person—and the treaty didn't say anything about people owning the moon or any planets. Mr. Hope filed a claim to the moon, Mars, and just about every known planet out there, and now he's making them available to you.

Getting rich takes creative thinking, and apparently there are enough people out there, who don't think at all, who are willing to part with enough money to make others rich. Why shouldn't that be you or me?

9

Going Through It

I have always been an entrepreneurial person, wanting to be my own boss for as long as I can remember. Although I've tried several times, I'm still just someone else's employee, not the employer. While exploring ideas for business ventures I pursued a career in the field I studied in college. I started my first business while I was still in college, however, and shut it down shortly after graduating. In college, I was a radical environmentalist, and I saw a need to tell "our" side of the story to as many people as the big corporations were able to reach. I was studying communications and broadcasting and used my skills and education to produce documentaries about environmental struggles throughout the country. "A clean environment is not wishful thinking" was my slogan.

The problem with this venture was that not many people were willing to pay to see these documentaries. (Would you pay to see *Toxic Roads: Warren County and Beyond?*) I then tried to get creative and packaged the videos with a "letter to your congressman." The idea was for people to buy the video and send me a letter, or use one of our generic ones, which I would send off to their senator or representative. This was before the anthrax attacks and before mail was X-rayed. This produced a few more sales, but I wasn't going to be able to *live* off this.

I wasn't willing to give up, though, and I did do some work for hire, producing videos for community groups or professional associations, but I didn't have the will or income to stick it out and see where it would lead. Here I was, still living with my parents, taking clients into my bedroom to show them rough edits of programs or examples of my work. This wouldn't work for long, but I certainly couldn't afford an office. Finally, I gave up and moved on, concentrating a bit more on my nine to five job.

An entrepreneur doesn't try just one thing; they keep trying until they find something that works. I figured there were other people who made documentaries and "alternative" programs, and they were doing well, so why not try to sell them? I could buy them at a discount and sell them at retail through a catalog.

The Catalog of Alternatives was born, and I sold vegetarian cookbooks, documentaries, and other independently produced videos. While I had some success, it was not enough to make it work, so I stopped this too.

As the years passed by, my career was going well, and my entrepreneurial spirit took some time off, but not too much time. By the time I was ready for my next business venture, the Internet was in full swing, and I wanted in. I had been using computers to network and find information before "internet" was a household word. I started on bulletin board systems, connecting by modem and using a computer that could display only text. (Remember the movie *War Games* with Mathew Broderick? That was me, sort of). I started Dig-it-all Productions to create websites for small businesses, but I was a bit too late.

Still not ready to give up on my entrepreneurial dream, I looked elsewhere for inspiration. My parents owned two houses in a resort town at the Jersey shore (okay, perhaps *resort* is a bit ambitious) and rented them out, one by the season and the other by the week. When I got old enough and had enough money to try this myself, my wife and I jumped in with both feet and bought a three-unit property. This would be my first successful business venture. We started a website for the house, and to our surprise, with no advertising expense, people found us through free listings with search engines.

The next business venture my wife and I would try grew from the vacation rental property. We wanted to do something special for our tenants as well as distinguish our rental property from others. We looked for affordable ideas, such as having small soaps imprinted with the name of our apartments, but couldn't find any. In my wife's searches, however, she found molds to make her own soap. All she had to do was melt some glycerin soap and pour it into the mold, so she tried it. She was very creative, using different colored soaps and layering the colors to create decorative soaps. The tenants loved them.

The soap business has done surprisingly well, bringing in approximately $700 to $1,400 per month in sales. This certainly isn't an amount we can live off, but we only do it part time, from home. We haven't even tried to branch out into stores, but that may be our next step. We haven't advertised other than in free listings and sales on eBay. Sometimes you find your next business idea and sometimes the idea finds you. We never intended to run a soap business, but the idea was there, so we decided to see where it would lead.

One day while I was sitting in front of my computer at work, a co-worker brought some chips into the edit room and offered me some. They were delicious! I had to ask for more, and I looked carefully at the bag for the name so I could get them for myself sometime. They weren't potato chips but pita chips,

Stacy's Pita Chips, to be exact. I had never heard of them, so I read the short history of the company on the back of the bag. Again, this was a business idea that wasn't developed as much as the idea found them. Here is what I read:

> Without the money to open a restaurant and with a passion for good food and a healthy lifestyle, Stacy and Mark (previously a social worker and psychologist) bought a Food Cart to serve healthy roll-up sandwiches.
> "We used the fresh pita bread from the sandwiches to make PITA CHIPS…what a hit!! As a benefit to standing in line for lunch, customers also got free chips!"
> Thus, Stacy's Pita Chip Company was born.

There are really only two things you need to succeed in business. The first is a belief in what you are doing. You not only have to believe what you're doing, but you have to believe it in the face of incredible opposition. But—and this is a big ol' but—there's a big difference in believing something and being too stubborn or too short sighted to see that it just won't work. I believed, and I still believe, in the documentaries I made with my video company, but I had to face the reality that without a viable market, my belief alone just wasn't enough.

The second quality you need to succeed in business is closely related to the first. If you truly believe that your idea is not only viable but necessary, then you have to have the will to stick it out and the passion to sell it to whomever you can. Ted Turner talks about CNN as if it was his child, as if he raised it from a baby into a successful adult—and in many ways he did. There's a glint in his eye when he talks about CNN, and it is then that you can see into his soul and know there was no way he could have failed. Of course, I'm saying this without ever meeting the man, but it's pretty evident from his various television interviews and profiles.

My wife and I are currently going through what many entrepreneurs have to go through when they start a new business. Will we be successful? I don't know, but we can't escape this truth: in order to succeed, we have to have all the same traits as the successful people I've described in these pages. Will we even want to succeed in the future? My wife has said that if she gets too busy making soap and has to hire help, she will give it up. That's too much responsibility, too much work on top of her full-time job.

You have to know that you can handle this type of stress and that you have the financial knowledge and discipline to succeed. People tend to make the same mistakes in business that they do in their personal lives. They don't communicate, they don't keep detailed records, and they don't make organization a top priority.

Other people will throw money at a problem instead of looking for a cheaper, albeit more difficult, solution.

I have a friend who runs a small side business that does quite well. I don't agree with some of his choices, however. One in particular stands out as a waste of money. The items he sold had bar codes, which he decided would be useful for tracking inventory. Until that point, he had been inputting the information into his computer manually. If he had a bar-code reader, he thought, this process would go much faster, saving him time to concentrate on other areas of the business.

His thinking was logical, but he ended up paying more than $600 for a bar-code system when he was doing just fine for free. The amount of money he spent would take a long time to recoup with his more "efficient" system of bar-coding every single item in stock.

As for my wife and me, our life, like yours, is a work in progress, and the information about us is subject to change at any moment. Maybe the soap business will become a much larger entity and one of us will quit our jobs to run it. Maybe we'll make some terrible mistakes or suffer some sort of tragedy that requires us to go into debt. Maybe the small amount of money my wife spends on the lottery (against my advice) will pay off and we won't have to work for anyone. The point is that you have to think about your finances as a flexible group of variables. What is true today might not be true tomorrow, but as long as you recognize that, you'll be fine. As long as you can adapt, you will be able to handle any circumstance.

10

Now What?

I hope that you're now thinking, "Hey, this is pretty good stuff." That would be nice, but you might also be wondering, "Can I actually do anything with this information?" Well, let's review. You should now have discipline and you should be able to keep track of your income and expenses. After taking the three-month test—no discretionary spending for three months—you will have seen where the waste is and will have corrected it. (Of course if it's taken you three months to get to this chapter then I've done something wrong). You can see where you can cut expenses if necessary and can apply what you've learned about the difference between want and need. You're willing to give up some things in order to get others. If you had credit card debt, you've begun to eliminate it completely. It might take a long time, but you're committed, because you know how much it will help you in the long run. If you can't do all of these things, then please go back and actually read the book. Don't just look at the words!

The next step is to decide what you want to do and then act on it. As I've said all along, I don't provide a list of rules you have to follow to become rich. What works for me might not work for you or anyone else, but common sense works for everyone. It doesn't take a genius to figure out that if you know where your money is coming from and going, you'll be in a better position to plan for the future. You don't have to have a 180 IQ to know that buying an expensive luxury car means you'll have to give up other things.

You should already see an improvement in your situation if you've followed the suggestions in this book. Now let's expand on these and talk about some of the common ways people try to make more money.

Below are things that people think they need to do to become wealthy. I hope I've shown you that there are other things you can do. Everyone wants the "eight-minute abs workout" of finances—the quick fix—but it ain't gonna happen. I think I've made my feelings clear about the get-rich-quick schemes out there.

One guy, Robert Allen, even claims to "have created more millionaires than any-one else, and he wants you to be next." Don't believe the hype (to steal a phrase)!

The Stock Market

That's what everyone has been waiting for, but it's taken me awhile to get here. Well, there's a reason for that. Just like there are pre-requisites in college, there are pre-requisites in personal finance. You can't run out and buy stock if you don't have a handle on the other aspects of your finances. I do not gamble at casi-nos, but I think of the stock market as my version of the roulette wheel. If I can't afford to lose the money I have in there, or have the time to recoup the losses, then I can't afford to play. I know it's a radical idea, but in light of the tech bub-ble and the virtual collapse of the stock market in 2001, it makes sense. I've seen too many people rely on their stock portfolio for almost everything, only to have to find a new way fast.

I'm not suggesting the bursting of the stock market bubble didn't affect me—it did, but that's my fault. The good news for me is that my losses didn't cause any financial hardship at all. If I actually sat down and calculated the return on my stock investments, I think I would find I was ahead. Certain accounts lost money, and others made money, but I certainly didn't get rich with the stock market. Actually, hold on a minute while I check the numbers.

. . . .

Thanks for waiting. It took a bit longer than I thought, because I just couldn't believe the numbers I was coming up with. In spite of actively managing my investments, I was shocked to learn that I have indeed lost money.

I can see people putting the book down as they read those words. What kind of a guide to getting rich is this if the author, the person you're trusting to help you, can't even help himself? You're not going to buy a book about the Internet written by a Mennonite. What must I have been thinking?

Once again, I have to remind you that simply because a successful person writes a book telling you that you can get rich doesn't mean you will. My success is made up of a series of failures and successes (although I hope there have been more successes) that together provide the basis of my future achievements. If I continue to make the same mistakes, I'm doomed to fail, but if I learn from my mistakes and modify my behavior, I will be that much closer to realizing my goals.

Can I offer you tricks to "win" in the stock market? No (obviously, I don't have any). Do I have a "system" that is sure to succeed? No. Do I have a hot "tip" for you, the next Microsoft? No. If someone or some book tells you they have some secret or great "system," throw it away and ignore that person. Remember common sense? Use it.

Now for the disclaimer about my losses. While it was true that when I did that calculation I told you about above, I had indeed lost money, that is no longer true. Here's the thing about writing a book. You don't sit down and write the whole thing in a day (although some books I've read sure sound as though the author did). Writing a book takes time, and for those aspiring writers out there like myself, who have no experience with the process, it takes even longer. A lot will change in the time it takes to finish writing a book. Case in point: my calculations now show that my investments have done quite nicely thank you very much. But the big secret is that I've done much better since I stopped chasing the latest hot stock or mutual fund. Instead of buying and selling stocks actively, I became a passive investor, buying only mutual funds—and index mutual funds at that. Read on and learn why this has been so much more beneficial than trying to find the next big thing.

If you're a follower of the stock market, the name Warren Buffet might sound familiar. Heck, even if you don't follow the stock market his name might sound familiar; after all, he is the second richest man in the world next to Bill Gates, and I've already mentioned Mr. Buffet in this book. He made his fortune through investments. Although he is a smart and successful stock picker, he has never owned Yahoo or Google! While everyone else was going crazy buying Internet stocks, Warren Buffet watched from the sidelines and stuck with his plan.

Sometimes he invests in companies as just another stockholder would, although he holds a lot more shares than you or I. Other times, he buys the entire company. His investments include Dairy Queen, Geico Insurance, Helzberg Diamonds, Fruit of the Loom, and many other companies. He owns stock in Coke and Gillette (now part of Proctor and Gamble) among other companies, but nothing very glamorous—no hot stock of the day. Furthermore, when he buys a stock, he waits a long time before he sells it. He doesn't believe in short-term investing. No, if he invests in a company, it's for the long haul through thick and thin. In a guide to investors, Buffet writes, "Gin rummy managerial behavior (discard your least promising business at each turn) is not our style. We would rather have our overall results penalized a bit than engage in that kind of behavior."

Another thing Warren Buffet doesn't believe in is stock splits. His investing company, Berkshire Hathaway, has never had a stock split; in 1981, you could have bought one share of the stock for $290, but as of this writing, just one share of his stock will cost you $89,000. Not many of us can afford to buy even one share of Berkshire Hathaway stock, but it's a good investment if you can. Just look at how it's grown over the years.

1981	$290 (very expensive then)
1982	$465
1983	$880
1984	$1,275
1985	$1,490
1986	$3,110
1987	$3,495
1988	$3,125
1989	$4,915
1990	$7,150
1991	$7,950
1992	$8,875
1993	$12,900
1994	$16,250
1995	$22,200
1996	$34,600
1997	$36,400
1998	$63,300
1999	$76,600
2000	$51,300 (what a bargain)
2001	$65,100
2002	$73,400
2003	$84,250
2004	$84,600
2005	$89,500 (as of this writing)

That is an impressive gain for one stock. The problem is that without splits, not many will be able to afford the stock, but that's fine with Mr. Buffet.

There are those who say investing based on the traditional measures of a stock is the old way of thinking. They say that in the new reality, people like Warren Buffet are out of touch, but I believe nothing is that stark—it's just not that easy. Sure, we as investors in a new millennium do have new ways to look at things, but when the clock struck midnight and the millennium changed, what was true the day before was still true then and the next day and the next day.

I mentioned earlier that Warren Buffet wrote a guide to investing in Berkshire Hathaway, which is posted on his website. This amazing document spells out his philosophy clearly and concisely and hasn't changed much since the day he wrote it. That's what I mean when I speak of discipline and consistency. Although there have been 27 amendments to the U.S. Constitution, the document hasn't changed much over the past two hundred twenty eight years. The system put in place in 1776 still works today. This is the reason Warren Buffet didn't jump on the Internet bandwagon, risking everything he worked so hard to get. "I've never believed in risking what my family and friends have and need," he wrote "in order to pursue what they don't have and don't need."

That is an important concept, and, if you've been paying attention, might sound a bit like the chapter called "Need vs. Want." Mr. Buffet, however, is talking about billions of dollars. How big of a risk are you willing to take to get something that you may not need (or even want) once you have it? Are you willing to quit your job and buy and sell real estate because you saw some testimonial on an infomercial?

Back to stocks. If I'm not going to give you a system or the next great company that will make you millions, what can I offer you? Mistakes. I can tell you about my mistakes and mistakes other people have made; it's then up to you not to make the same errors we have. I'll also tell you what seems to work for me, but I'm not making any promises. ***Promises are the tool of the con artist.***

I can't tell you how many times I've bought a stock I believed in and then bought more when the price dipped, thinking I was getting a bargain. I did this with one stock in particular. It was a huge name, and I never thought it could go under. I first bought it at over $70 a share and then it split, and I thought I was on my way to riches. The stock went down a bit, so I bought some more and told others to do the same. It went down a little more, and then some more, and suddenly the bottom just fell out. The stock was Lucent Technologies, and while it hasn't gone bankrupt, I have lost almost every penny I put into it. The stock is now around $3 a share.

I have had other successful stock purchases that have gone terribly wrong as well. After I bought Lucent and it split, things were looking good, but I got greedy and thought there were only profits ahead. I've had stocks that were up 30 percent or more and then watched them drop to 60 percent below my purchase price.

This brings me to the subject of math. I always questioned the need to understand more than simple addition, subtraction, multiplication, and division when I was in school, but now I know why my teachers were right. Let me give you a simple real-world example. Let's say you bought a stock that went up 80 percent. You'd be pretty happy with your stock-picking ability and would probably brag to all your friends about how smart you are—I know I would. But say you picked up the paper one morning to read that the main product this company made was defective and would have to be recalled. The stock now drops 50 percent. Are you worried? I mean, you were up 80 percent, right? Are you ahead, or have you lost money? I'll give you a minute to think about it.

Okay, time's up. What was your answer? If you thought you were still a bit ahead, you would be wrong. This time, let's attach some dollar figures to the example. You buy a stock for $100, and it increases 80 percent, so now it's worth $180. That's a nice gain—congratulate yourself. But now you open the paper, read the bad news, and see that the stock has dropped 50 percent from when the stock market opened, so now it's worth only $90. That's $10 less than you paid for it. You've lost 10 percent. It is this reality that has lead me to change my strategy, and it seems to be working.

Let's assume I find a stock I like—say, TiVo, the digital video recording system. I bought TIVO for about $7 a share and watched it quickly climb to $9, then $11, and then finally over $13 a share. I was no longer going to watch profits like that slip away as the stock pulled back to $7 or less, and so I sold half of my investment at $12 a share, for a profit of 71 percent, or $5 a share. I kept half my investment in case the stock kept going up, but if it somehow dropped to nothing, I wouldn't be as bad off as I would have had I gotten greedy and held onto the stock. My next target was $14. If the stock reached $14, I would sell half of what I had left for a profit on those shares of 100 percent. So far, that hasn't happened, but I have a backup plan, too. If the stock slips back down to $8, I'm going to sell all of it. This way I've lost nothing. The converse is also true, however, and my wife has been vindicated on this one. I sold all our TIVO shares at about $8.75, and sure enough they dropped further, but then they slowly made their way back up and are at almost $11 again (at the time of this writing; if they're higher than that when you read this, my wife likely hates me). You win some and lose some, but taking the profits when I did insured that they were real profits.

Let's take another example that my wife likes to point to as a reason to hold onto stocks no matter how high (or low) they get. We bought Amazon.com for about $9 a share and watched it rise rather quickly to $18, then over $20 a share. We had made over 100 percent profit in a short period, and with my newfound sense of discipline, I wasn't about to let this one slip away. I decided enough was enough and sold the whole lot for a profit of over 115 percent. Not bad, but had I held onto them until today, I would have made over 300 percent in profits. I still think I made the right decision—I made money, and who can argue with that?

Have you noticed that I'm giving you percentages and not actual dollar amounts of my investments? Well, there's a reason for that: I don't want you to know how much money I have! Well, that's not entirely true. It's just that percentages give you a more accurate picture of what a person makes or loses. Assume that I bought Amazon.com for $9 a share and sold it for a profit of a million dollars. That sounds like a great profit, but what if I had bought a million shares? Then my gain would have been only $1, or a little more than 10 percent.

This last example brings me to a sad but true fact. The more money you have, the more money you can make. I say "can" and not "will," because it is also true that the more money you have, the more you can lose. If that same person bought a million shares of Amazon.com and the price went down to $8 a share, they would have lost a million dollars. They still have eight million dollars in the stock, but they have lost a million. That's bad no matter how you look at it.

The stock market is just one way to increase your net worth without manual labor but don't think that quitting your job and becoming a day trader is a good idea. Maybe there are other ways you can make your fortune.

Real Estate

If you think I'm going to tell you how to buy houses and sell them for a quick profit, you haven't been reading up to this point. It is true that real estate is a great way to make money. You can even feel justified going into debt to buy property (within reason). This does not mean that you should mortgage yourself to the hilt just to buy a big, beautiful house because it's a good investment. Don't forget about the interest you're paying. As in any other business, to make money in real estate, you have to bring in more money than you put out.

The people who will tell you that your home is actually a bad investment like to cite the fact that you're paying property taxes and an exorbitant amount of interest. The question is, "What's the alternative?" You have to live somewhere, and no matter where it is, you'll have to pay something. Let's assume you're paying rent. Are you paying property taxes and interest? Well, not directly, but you can be sure that the property owner is charging enough to cover those expenses, so in a sense you are.

Let me use my rental house at the beach as an example to illustrate the true cost of owning a home. I put $50,000 down on the total cost of $225,000 for the house. My mortgage from day one was $175,000. If someone offered me $200,000 the next day, I would lose money, even though that is $25,000 more than I owed on that day. I know that's obvious, and I don't mean to insult your, what's the word, smartness. Now, let's project ten years down the road and assume that someone offered me $275,000. That certainly seems like a good deal, considering that I only spent $225,000. It looks like a $50,000 profit, but not so fast! After you take into account the interest I've paid ($30,000), I'm actually only making $20,000. That's not a bad amount, but it also isn't the $50,000 you thought it was. Don't forget the property taxes I've paid as well. All of this goes into the formula when figuring out if you truly made any money.

In the example above you were left with a $20,000 profit. But assume you had a lot of credit card debt and, in order to reduce that burden, you took out a home equity loan for $50,000 that was used to pay off those cards. Now that $20,000 profit has turned into a $30,000 loss. Real estate is a good investment, but it requires work. In this example, in spite of the large home equity loan, you will actually have money in your pocket when the sale is final. You've paid down the principal for ten years and therefore owe less than your original purchase price. Let's assume that on the date of sale, you owe $175,000. This means that after you pay off the home equity loan I spoke of earlier, you'll actually have $50,000 in proceeds from the sale. However, what you have now doesn't matter; it's what you've spent over the years that counts. What I mean is this: if you hadn't gotten into trouble with your credit cards and needed that home equity loan, you would have pocketed $100,000 when you sold the house. Of course, some people just think they're doing okay because they have some cash in hand and don't think about how much more they would have if they had been a bit more careful with their money.

Back to my rental house. I spent $225,000, putting $50,000 down, and in the few short years I owned it, I spent $30,000 in interest and paid the principal down by $10,000, leaving me with a balance of $165,000 owed. When I add the interest payments to the cost of the house, so far I've spent $255,000 out of pocket. Now add in the utility bills and maintenance/repair costs, and you'll see that the house has really cost me $270,000. If someone offered me $270,000, the easy calculation would produce a profit of $45,000, but as I've just shown, I would really only break even.

Not missing a thing, you ask me "This is a rental property isn't it?" to which my only response can be, "Yes it is." This means I had income to offset the expenses. Once you add that income into the equation, you'll see that the offer of $270,000 leaves me with a profit of $30,000. Not bad, but still not as much as the easy calculation, which would give me a profit of $45,000.

My wife and I do the repairs and remodeling ourselves, working almost every weekend we can. Hiring someone to do the work would eat into our profit. Other people might not be able to do the amount of work we do or might not be willing to give up what we do in order to save the money. This is what I mean when I say it takes work to become rich (and we're not rich—yet—at least not in our eyes). This is what it means to make choices. I would have liked to relax some weekends, but if I want to get ahead, that's not always possible. I know there will be plenty of time for that in the future—if things go as planned.

There was another problem with our rental house, one that is actually an advantage for many people who have rental income. Most people who own real estate that they rent can deduct from their taxes the mortgage interest and the cost of repairs (at least for the portion of the home they rent), but we could not. This deduction is what's called a tax shelter, because it allows you to shelter that money in the house—you receive a tax deduction while building the value of the home. The problem was that my wife and I made too much money. Once you make more than $150,000 a year, you can no longer deduct those costs right away. Instead, you carry them over year after year, until you sell the house. When you sell the house, those accumulated expenses are then deducted from the capital gain on the sale. You still get the deduction, just not right away.

It's important to remember that there are no simple answers to questions of money. If you think simply—for example, "Real estate is a good investment"—without thinking about potential problems like the one I outlined above, then you are going to fail. Or at least you will not do as well as you could have.

I'll give you another example that illustrates how to look at a financial decision from multiple angles. I know I keep using my rental property as an example, but hey, it's all I got—give me a break. Another tax advantage to owning investment real estate is that you can depreciate it over time. The depreciation schedule set by the IRS is 27.5 years. Basically, you take the purchase price and divide by 27.5, and that's what you can deduct each year. When I purchased the property, all three apartments were fully furnished. I knew that when you buy furniture and other improvements, the depreciation schedule is much faster for those items (five to seven years) than it is for the actual structure.

The first thing I did was call my accountant and asked him, "If I structure the purchase price of the house as follows: $205,000 for the dwelling and $20,000 for the furniture, can we depreciate the furniture faster, thereby resulting in a savings that much quicker?" The answer was yes, and that is exactly what I did. Had I not looked for that slight advantage, I would have done the easy thing and simply included the furniture in the total purchase price. I would have missed out.

The point of all this is that if you are willing to put in the time to find property that can make you money, and if you are willing to put some hard work into it, then, yes, real estate is a good investment, but it certainly isn't as easy as they make it seem on the Saturday-morning infomercials.

Speaking of the infomercials, just how do they think you're going to buy a house and sell it within a month for a profit of $40,000? The answer is foreclosures. That's right, these systems have you prey on other people's misfortune, but that's the way the system works, so there really isn't anything wrong with buying properties that are being foreclosed. The problem with these plans is that they just aren't as easy as the infomercial pitch men say they are.

Here's one way it works. When a house is foreclosed, it is auctioned off at a sheriff's sale in the county where the property is located. You may have seen the ads in the local paper's legal notice section.

SHERIFF'S FILE NO. 2002-513227
SHERIFF'S SALE
SUPERIOR COURT OF NEW JERSEY, CHAN-
CERY DIVISION, ESSEX COUNTY, DOCKET NO.
F2172181 GMAC MORTGAGE CORPORATION,
PLAINTIFF -vs- ████████████████ ET AL. DE-
FENDANTS Execution For Sale of Mortgaged
Premises
    By virtue of the above stated writ of Execution, to
me directed, I shall expose for sale by Public Auction,
in SHERIFF'S OFFICE, Essex County Courts Build-
ing in Newark, on Tuesday, August 19, 2003, at one-
thirty P.M. (Prevailing Time)
Commonly known as:
0000000042█████████████
NEWARK NJ 07106
Lot:█ Block: 4126
Size: 40.00' X 85.00' X 40.00' X 85.00'
Nearest cross street name: ANDOVER PLACE
    A full legal description can be found in the office of
the Register of Essex County.
    A deposit of 20% of the bid price in certified funds is
required at the time of sale.
The approximate amount of the Judgment to be sa-
tisfied by said sale is the sum of ONE HUNDRED
FORTY NINE THOUSAND SIX HUNDRED SIXTY
FOUR AND 97/100 DOLLARS ($149,664.97), together
with the costs of this sale.
    The Sheriff reserves the right to adjourn the sale
from time to time as provided by Law.
                    Newark, N.J. July 14, 2003
            ARMANDO B. FONTOURA, Sheriff
        PLUESE, ETTIN, BECKER & SALTZMAN,
                            ATTORNEY(S)
Pub: July 23, 30, August 6, 13, 2003 $246.00

Anyone can go to the auction and bid on the property, with the highest bid being the purchase price. Although the procedure is slightly different depending on the particular county's laws, 20 percent of the winning bid is usually due on the spot. This means if you have won a bid for $40,000 then you had better have $8,000 in cash (or more likely a certified check) with you. The house is not yours yet. Now you have thirty days to come up with the rest of the money and deal with other issues, such as the title and getting the current owners out. Once the house is yours, you can list it for sale and sell it quickly for a profit.

This sounds easy, and I've seen advocates of this scheme claim that they have done this with six houses in only five hours of work. Five hours sounds low to me. Taking risks can pay off, but if you can reduce the risk, do it. If you want to ensure there is as little risk as possible, you have to do a bit more work than just show up at the auction.

If someone has lost their house in a foreclosure and it's gotten to the point of a sheriff's sale, they probably have other money problems too. This means there might be liens against the property. As the purchaser of the property at auction, you are responsible for paying these liens. This means that before you bid, you had better be darn sure that what you pay is really what you'll owe. To do this, you will have to make a few phone calls and spend some money. You'll have to call the local tax collector and find out if there are any back taxes owed on the property. You should also do a title search to find out if there are any liens. Who would put a lien on someone's property? Well, there could be back taxes owed, or it could have been a contractor who did some work but was never paid, or it could be a utility company that wasn't paid. Wouldn't you want to know this before you put your 20 percent non-refundable deposit down at auction?

There's another problem with this scheme. The numbers sound great, but what kind of house are you going to get for $40,000? It's probably not in a great neighborhood, or it has been neglected. The chances are that the property will need some work. That's not to say that you can't sell it for a profit to someone else who is willing to do the work, but finding such a person just adds another layer of difficulty.

Real Estate Secrets Revealed

Are you salivating? Are you excited, thinking you are about to receive information nobody else has? Well, if anyone, and that includes me, tells you they will reveal a secret to wealth or investing, you can be sure of two things: they aren't going to tell you much, and what they're telling you isn't such a secret after all. I have a personal story to relate as an example.

I am constantly looking for information. I'm constantly searching for good ideas to educate myself in the methods used to invest in real estate. One particular website offered its members the opportunity to participate in a conference call to learn a "secret that would eliminate 90 percent of [their] competition" in the pre-foreclosure business. The call was free, and I was willing to spend the 45 minutes or so listening in.

I dialed the number, and the presentation began right on time. The speaker began with an introduction and some background on his qualifications. He took extra care to point out that he still invests in and makes his money in real estate. This struck me as odd, since the topic of his talk was real estate investing. What did he think we thought he did to make money?

He began by giving quite a bit of background on this "secret." I couldn't wait to hear it; there were quite a few real estate investors out there, and I would think someone else would know about such a successful strategy.

Finally, when the moment came to reveal the secret, it was how he had discovered the secret that amazed me. Was it on a conference call, where someone had promised to tell him a secret, much as he had promised me? No. Did he pay an exorbitant amount of money to buy the secret? No again. This secret, which was so amazing that only a select few were invited onto the conference call to hear it, came from a mortgage banker who simply told it to him, as he was simply telling us. When he mentioned the name of the secret, a mortgage workout, I immediately did a search for the term on Google and discovered it wasn't all that secret after all.

So here I was on the phone, hearing a secret that many people seemed to know about already, when the real purpose of the conference call became clear. The speaker was willing to train us in the techniques he just told us about in order to flatten the learning curve. Sure, we could put this secret to work on our own, but why spend the time researching and learning the "hard way" when he's already done all the leg work? It made sense, and for just $1,495 I could be making money and eliminating my competition. But wait! That was just the usual price for the class; if you called the special toll-free number and signed up right now, it would cost only $495. Of course, this was only open to the first thirty people, so if I didn't want to be left out, I'd have to call now. I did not call.

After a simple forty-five minute presentation, this man was making (if all thirty people signed up) over $14,000, and all he was going to do was provide access to an online course and send you all the training material. So, how do you think he makes most of his money? Real estate or selling secrets to people who want easy money?

The point of this book is not to teach you how to invest in real estate, play the stock market, start a business, or open a franchise. The point is to let you know that you can do better if you want to and, more importantly, that as long as you use some common sense, you don't need someone else to tell you what to do. You certainly don't need them to sell you access to a secret that turns out not to be such a secret after all.

Starting Your Own Business

Taking the plunge and going into business for yourself is a great idea, and although it's not true that you can't get rich working for someone else, you can increase your chances if you go it alone. You will also increase your chances of losing everything if you do it without the proper preparation. Like everything else in life, and therefore in this book, it's not going to be easy to start your own business.

It's not enough simply to make choices; they must be informed choices. If you have to guess, then make it an educated guess. If you work hard and educate yourself, you'll probably do all right. You'll at least minimize the impact of wrong decisions.

Since, as I've stated above, I'm in the midst of starting my own business, I might not be the best person to give you advice on this topic, but who are the best people to tell you how to start your own business? People who have done it! That makes sense, doesn't it? But some are better than others. Bill Gates started his own business, but I don't think he's a good example. The issues related to starting Microsoft don't easily translate to a smaller venture. We're not looking to go to those heights, although I wouldn't complain about having a few billion dollars to play with.

How about one of those Internet millionaires? No, that's not really a good example either. They just don't seem real enough yet. Their stocks are still valued higher than their profits seem to indicate. Only time will tell if that type of business is something that we can count on in the future.

How about people who make money using the Internet but aren't technology companies like Microsoft or Yahoo!? I'm thinking specifically of people who sell items on eBay. While it's true there are some people making a fortune doing just that, only selling on eBay seems too limiting. For our purposes, I'm thinking of something more tangible.

A store, a physical location, is what most people think of when they hear that someone is opening a business. Whether it's an office or a retail outlet, people think of "bricks and mortar" to use an over-used term. Now that I've put the idea of an actual structure in your mind, I'll tell you what I think is a great example of a successful business. Not that I was intentionally steering you in the wrong direction but my idea lies somewhere between a traditional manufacturer and an internet company. It relies on a traditional business model while using the internet to reach customers. What could be more traditional than making something and selling it? Any item that can be manufactured, such as a candle or a set of dishes, would work, but I'm thinking of a computer. The manufacturing business model is the same for any product. You need a factory, whether you are producing computers or candles, but it's how you sell your product that makes a difference.

Michael Dell (of Dell computers) saw a product that was already available, the computer, and decided he would sell them too. His sales model was what gave him the advantage, although it wasn't entirely new. Just-in-time manufacturing was a known concept before Michael (like we're on a first name basis) began Dell Computers.

Mr. Dell began his business while still attending college and sold computers from his dorm room (definitely a bricks and mortar structure). Instead of starting with a huge warehouse, he expanded as quickly as the market allowed but did not (and this is important) get ahead of himself. He started with a small office that he soon outgrew rather than a big office that he could grow into. Today, he is the largest seller of personal computers in the world.

Can you do the same thing Michael Dell did? Maybe. Remember, it doesn't matter what the product is as long as you can sell it better than your competition. Soap doesn't sound like a wonderful product to make and sell, but so far my wife and I (mostly my wife) have given people a unique item with a personal touch. It's that personal touch that matters. Now we are faced with the prospects of growing larger and have to ask ourselves some important questions, such as, *How big do we want to get?* You have to ask yourself this first, and then work toward that goal.

Financial Advisors

Once you understand money and can control yourself, you'll begin to build wealth. How you do that is up to you, but any of the above examples, from starting a business to investing in real estate, are a good start. Let's assume you've done well and now, instead of not knowing how to retain savings, you don't know what to do with all that money you have. It's a problem most people think they want. What do you do?

The richer you are, the more help you will need managing your money. It can become a full-time job. But even on a smaller scale, getting help is not a bad idea. Finding a plan that works and sticking with it will also help you become more disciplined.

You might think I'm letting you off easy on this one, but like everything else in life—and in this book—it just isn't that easy. Look at Mike Tyson. He had financial advisors and he still somehow lost 300 million dollars. Billy Joel had money problems, and just look at some of the child actors from your favorite TV shows. Some of them are in sad shape. The point is, you have to find the right kind of advisor for your type of money.

"Money is money, isn't it?" you ask.

"No" I reply, shaking my head as if you haven't read any of the book.

Maybe everything is going well and all you need to do is re-examine your current situation and tweak it a bit. Maybe you need a full-time money manager. Maybe you need a little of both, some basic advice and someone to manage the investment portion of your money. Just as there are different types of lawyers—tax attorneys, criminal attorneys, and patent attorneys, etc.—there are different types of financial advisors.

Financial advisors fit into three basic categories: commission only, fee only, and hybrid, a mixture of the two. When my wife and I decided it would be a good idea to consult a financial advisor, we chose the latter, and it worked out well for a while.

A commission-only financial advisor doesn't charge any fees to the client, such as plan set-up fees. They make their money by selling you products that make them a commission. You might want to buy XYZ mutual fund, but they will try to sell you ABC mutual fund because they make a commission. A fee-only financial advisor is the polar opposite of a commission-only advisor. They will collect a fee from the client, usually based on a percentage of assets managed, but will never earn commissions on what they sell you. It's as simple as this, if your assets increase they will do better. What better incentive is there than that? Let's say you have $100,000 to invest and you use a fee-only advisor. He charges 1.25 percent, so the first year, you give him $1,250 as his fee. Now the next year rolls around, and your portfolio is now worth only $90,000. It was a bad year. Your advisor will still get his fee, but this time it will only be $1,125. If instead of losing money, your investments were worth $110,000 the next year, the advisor would get $1,375. You did better, and so did he.

A hybrid advisor is simply a combination of the two. In our case, he charged us a fee to set up our "plan" and then sold us items that made him a commission. The initial fee was fairly small (under $300), and the commissions were invisible to me; in other words, the commissions were hidden in the cost of the investments he was selling me. This worked well for a little while, because once the plan was complete we did most of our buying and selling on our own, only occasionally buying mutual funds through our advisor.

Things went wrong when I asked him to research a specific type of investment I was interested in. I, of course, had done my own investigation and found several mutual funds that looked promising. The advisor, however, came up with a stock I had never heard of as an alternative and pushed hard for me to buy it. When I insisted that we buy my choice of mutual fund, he refused, since there was no commission for him. That's when our relationship ended.

We have since removed all of our accounts from that advisor's control, and we have yet to hire a new one. We have streamlined our accounts, however, helping us to keep things a bit more organized.

Another thing to look out for is advisors who try to sell you insurance. If you want to buy insurance go, to an insurance company, and if you want investment advice, go to a financial advisor, and may the two never meet. There may be occasions when you can use insurance as an investment, but only under very specific circumstances, so be suspicious if a financial advisor tries to sell you insurance.

There are entire books devoted to each topic in this book. Use the advice you find here as a starting point. Dealing with finances is not something you ever become an expert on. I may know what I'm talking about—that's for you to decide—but I'm still learning every day. I watch television shows devoted to the subject because I don't know it all. I read books, websites, and postings by people I don't know so I can find a better way of doing things.

Everything in this book has come from my experiences, from my constant desire to educate myself and work toward my goals. The information I've gathered has come from the very sources you should be looking at. If you think you know it all and therefore stop looking for better solutions to your everyday financial problems, you'll never live up to your full potential. This is your new job. From now on, you are your own financial advisor, whether or not you also have outside advisors.

11

Death and Taxes

If you do nothing else in life, there are only two certainties: death and taxes. Taxes aren't certain, but who am I to ruin such a famous saying. Perhaps you've heard the story of someone who was jailed for tax evasion. After emerging from prison, they said, "I worked so hard for that money I thought it was mine." A lot of people think the same way, but they're wrong—it's only mostly theirs.

My father hates taxes. Many of the authors of financial books sound like they hate taxes too. I don't particularly like them, but I do feel an obligation to pay my fair share. People seem to be most upset that some are getting a free ride while the most successful foot the bill. You may be a pure capitalist and expect everyone to fend for themselves, letting the least fortunate live in abject poverty, but that's not for me.

It's true my father always complains about taxes (even ones he will never pay, such as the estate tax) and just doesn't understand me whenever we discuss the subject. "Rich loves to pay taxes," he says. When I complain about taxes or tell him about some legal loophole I might be using, he says, "But I thought you loved taxes?"

No dad, I don't like taxes, but I do like the protection of a strong military and the safe streets provided by the police and fire department. I like that the roads I drive on are paved and maintained. They could be better, but they could be a lot worse, too. I like the fact that when I reach retirement age, even if I've messed up badly, I'll still have social security and Medicare and Medicaid (in spite of all the gloom and doom to the contrary). I like the fact that we, as a nation, have land set aside for us, and our future generations, to enjoy. Do I want to pay more taxes than I have to? No, but do I want someone with less income than me to pay my share toward the freedom I enjoy?

Are taxes fair? Probably not, but I don't think they ever can be. Someone will always pay more than the rest, while others will "get a free ride." Imagine that there were no deductions or tax shelters, that you simply have to pay whatever your tax bracket indicated. This would mean that if you were in the highest tax bracket (currently 35 percent, for incomes of $319,100 or more), you would pay $111,685 in taxes. That's a lot of money, but you would be left with $207,415, and I just don't understand how anyone can complain about that. Someone with a middle-class salary, making $50,000 a year, would be in the 25 percent tax bracket and would pay $12,500 in taxes, leaving them with $37,500. It would be nice to keep all of it, but as I said earlier, you are getting certain protections in return for your taxes.

People who complain about taxes being too high will often state that 1 percent of the people pay 80 percent of the taxes. While this is somewhat true, as I said earlier, statistics don't tell the whole truth. That same 1 percent makes 70 percent of the money in this country. That means that the other 99 percent combined—including me, and probably you—only makes 30 percent of all the money in this country. If there was anything that wasn't fair, this is it.

But what does this have to do with you? How does this affect your wealth? I believe that people spend way too much time thinking about how to avoid taxes or will make a bad decision just because they can save a little on their taxes. I've given the example of investing in real estate as a way to shelter some money from taxes but in my case, I wasn't able to do that. If I was counting on this "savings" then I may have caused myself more harm than good.

There's a lot of talk recently about eliminating the mortgage deduction. People often talk about the tax advantage of owning a home but a tax deduction is no reason to make a financial decision. The mortgage deduction is no bargain, you're paying one dollar to get twenty eight cents back. Where's the logic in that?

Another thing someone might do is borrow money from their 401(k) rather than take a more conventional loan since that was money they never paid taxes on and the interest they have to pay goes right back into their 401(k). I don't think you'll find a financial advisor or author who would ever advocate taking money, even a loan, from your 401(k).

It's one thing to try to minimize your tax burden but quite another to constantly complain about something we all have to pay. Concentrate on the things you can change and not on those you can't.

12

Good Luck and Keep Learning

I suppose I could drag things out a bit longer, telling you things that sound good but that won't really help you. I could fill you up with statistics, give you a pep talk, or regale you with stories of my youth but I'll spare you the suffering. The book is over, and I could leave it at that, too, but something is telling me to keep going (and I wish it would stop).

I don't think I've missed an opportunity to remind you that I think most personal finance books out there don't offer much in the way of useful information. I hope I have. I hope you will be more successful because of this book. I hope you will think differently and smartly when it comes to the financial decisions you make every day of your life. You can lie, put on airs, and project an image of success, but, in the end, you have to answer to yourself.

I don't do lists, remember, but I will cover some of the finer moments in the book for you now.

It's Monday morning. You've just finished reading this book and want to begin your new life. The first thing you do is eat breakfast, because somewhere in these pages I said it was the most important meal of the day, and you believed me. While eating, you begin your first assignment. You sit down at the computer and begin setting up your financial tracking application. You might think you're good with money, but you know that keeping detailed records will give you much more of an advantage. It's what separates those who fly by the seat of their pants from those who can navigate the murky waters with precision.

It doesn't take too long, and now you can find all of your financial information in one place. The next thing you do is test yourself. Maybe you have credit card debt or just can't understand where your money goes every month, so you've decided to take a stand. You will take three months out of your spending life in order to prepare yourself for a lifetime of success. You understand that prosperity takes work and that luck simply isn't enough. Today, you have decided that you believe in yourself and can't (and won't) rely on dreams to improve your financial situation. Goodbye lottery, hello hard (but satisfying) work.

If credit card debt is a problem and you have more than two cards, you will cut up (but not cancel) all but the two most necessary. You leave for work knowing that you own the credit cards; they don't own you. Sooner than you can imagine, debt will be a distant memory and you will have something you thought was impossible, positive cash flow.

You know that what's important today will not necessarily be important in the future. ***Live every day as if it's your last; just don't spend money that way.*** In order to get ahead, you realize that you can't always get what you want (to quote Mick Jagger). If you ask yourself if you really need something rather than just want it, you'll be a much better consumer. If you realize you aren't what you drive or what you wear, that there's more to you than material things, you'll be able to afford what truly makes you happy rather than what makes you look happy.

On your way to work, maybe you take a train or a bus, and you notice a *Wall Street Journal*, *Forbes*, *Money*, or *Smart Money* magazine someone has left behind. You decide that you will be a more educated person and so you read it. This book is one of many that you will read, knowing why one is better than the other and sifting through the junk in order to find little jewels of information that will make you a richer person.

While you're at work, perhaps a little bored or maybe just tired of not getting the recognition you deserve, you decide to put in some overtime (if you get it) or go for that promotion (or both) so you will be better able to pursue your dream. Working for someone else might not be the best choice, but it's all you have right now. You know that someday the right opportunity will come by, and you want to be in a position to grab it.

Whatever choices you make, I hope they're right for you. I hope that success finds you well. Good luck in the future, and may you earn all your dreams.

And you thought the book was over but no, I just keep going and going. If you've been paying attention then you know that I believe that if I tell you something, I ought to give you concrete evidence to back up my position. Therefore, if I tell you that there's a lot of good information out there, I suppose I had better tell you where it is.

We all know that CNBC is *the* source on television for financial news and information, and I think it's the best (but remember, I sort of worked there once). Watch it to learn the terminology and big-picture concepts, but don't expect to find the next Microsoft or learn when the next market crash will happen. The problem is that while it's a good source of information, you shouldn't watch it thinking you'll find the next great stock tip that will make you millions. I've seen people give advice about one stock or another and be right, and I've seen people be completely wrong (those are the stocks I usually bought). You might think they're experts and trust every word they say, but you would be wrong to do so. The good thing about the anchors and hosts on CNBC is that they tell you when people do really stupid things. For example, they often point out when a broker or brokerage downgrades a stock *after* it has lost most of its value or upgrades it *after* it has gained a huge amount of value. The point I'm trying to make is this: just because you see it on TV or read it in a book or magazine doesn't mean it's true. Even the experts are late to the game once in a while. You have to do your own research if you really want to be sure.

Read! Read books, magazines, newsletters, websites, and web forums. Read *The Millionaire Next Door*. Read anything by Suze Orman. Watch *The Suze Orman Show* on CNBC. It has to be the best and most (brutally) honest show out there. Read *Smart Money* magazine. Go to www.motleyfool.com and spend days, weeks, and even months reading everything you possibly can. Use their forums section to see what other people, who have been through what you are going through now, have to say. Go to my blog at www.richeobscure.com and see what other nonsense I've come up with. There you'll also find a much more comprehensive list of links to yet more information. Now you know that information is the most powerful tool at your disposal.

And now for the final words you'll read: enjoy your success. Thank you.

978-0-595-37233-1
0-595-37233-3

www.ingramcontent.com/pod-product-compliance
Lightning Source LLC
Chambersburg PA
CBHW030911180526
45163CB00004B/1789